"*The Thinking Parent* offers a range of practical, common sense ideas for parents of school-age children to think about in regard to such important areas as self-esteem, moral development, developing internal control, discipline, and motivation to learn. Rather than offering "quick fixes," this useful book describes basic suggestions for action that apply to many everyday situations and help to build the long-term parent-child relationship."

Betty Cooke, Ph.D.
Early Childhood Family Education Specialist
Minnesota Department of Education

"*The Thinking Parent* is respectful and supportive of parents, yet challenges them to be the best parents that they can be. Stokes blends knowledge about child development with a first-hand experience of parenting issues. The stories and anecdotes make this an easy book to read. The summary tables at the end of each chapter make the parenting advice easy to access.

"The tone of the book is optimistic and hopeful without belittling or oversimplifying the task of parenting. Parents will find this book a rich resource of ideas and practical advice as they undertake the exhausting and exhilarating task of guiding their children through their school years."

Glen F. Palm
Associate Professor of Child and Family Studies
St. Cloud State University

"Open, friendly, and conversational in tone, *The Thinking Parent* fills a vacuum in books for mothers and fathers of elementary school children. Anne Stokes features what most books on parenting leave out...the moral development of the child, including empathy, internal control and common courtesy. She demonstrates how to build a cohesive family, not just a collection of individuals. Helpful summaries end each chapter and down-to-earth examples abound throughout the book."

Dr. Martha Miller
Educational Policy Analyst
Florida Department of Education

"*The Thinking Parent* is an important resource for child rearing. Stokes reveals a warm sympathy for both parents and children, plus a confident style that establishes her competence as a writer. She understands the whole child, who is nurtured out of the life values of a family.

"The book's clarity reflects the deep knowledge and experience of Anne Stokes, who offers positive, practical suggestions and an outline summary in each chapter. It will encourage and strengthen parents because they will sense that she has shared the task and found it rewarding."

Iris V. Cully
Professor Emerita, Christian Education
Lexington Theological Seminary

ANNE STOKES

THE THINKING PARENT

Understanding and Guiding Your Child

a division of
TWENTY-THIRD PUBLICATIONS
Mystic CT 06355

Twenty-Third Publications
185 Willow Street
P.O. Box 180
Mystic CT 06355
(203) 536-2611
800-321-0411

© Copyright 1993 Anne Stokes. All rights reserved. No part of this publication may be reproduced in any manner without prior written permission of the publisher. Write to Permissions Editor.

ISBN 0-89622-568-2
Library of Congress Catalog Card Number 93-60401

Foreword

Several years ago when my wife and I were sitting on the patio drinking our morning coffee, she suddenly looked at me and said, "Carl, are we going to make it?" I knew immediately that she was talking about raising our children and surviving—much less thriving—as a family. I responded, "Of course we're going to make it." She demanded reassurance: "How can you be so sure?" I explained, "Because millions of others before us have made it." We are living in a different world today. The traditional family structure has taken on different, varied forms over recent decades, but parents are the same: they still want the best for their children.

But what is "the best"? Parenting in the 1990s is a challenging, even a daunting task. It seems that none of us has the time, the energy, the creativity, or the support that the job demands. We're always looking for "answers," that elusive formula that will guide us unerringly to produce happy, productive children. Of course, even the parents of infants have discovered in the middle of the night that there are no magic tricks. In fact, successful parenting today demands more resourcefulness than in times past, and parents are seeking help wherever they can.

In my years as both a father and a public educator, I've seen many traditional supports for parents disappear. The advantage of grandparents close at hand, the neighbor-to-neighbor approach, the luxury of enough daylight hours for family activities are gone for most families. Communities that used to revolve around children now have critical concerns about issues such as changing demographics, personal safety, health care, chemical use, homelessness, lack of affordable day care, and more.

In these stressful times, Anne Stokes has been a leader in creating new supports for parents. As coordinator of the nationally-recognized Time Out Together School (TOTS) in St. Louis Park, Minnesota, since 1978, she has worked with staff and parents to develop a program that strengthens families, teaches parenting skills, and provides children with age-appropriate experiences. Modeling effective parenting techniques, TOTS helps build positive family situations that enable preschool children to reach their potential, including the ability to profit socially and academically from future school experiences.

In short, TOTS brings parents and children to a central community center where they can recreate a neighborhood feeling. Parents can share with other mothers and fathers their questions, anxieties, proud stories, and funny snapshots. They can learn about stages of child development that earlier generations could observe by watching a neighborhood full of children out their kitchen windows. They can learn about the importance of play in developing children's skills in language, dexterity, and cooperation with others. Both parents and children can learn that it's all right to try and fail and to try again. Children, from birth to kindergarten age, learn to explore and grow in Time Out Together School playrooms.

The quality of parenting affects more than the success of individual children. The effectiveness of today's parents as their children's first and most important teachers is of critical importance to the success of our future in this country.

Foreword

Schools are being asked to do more and more—and without parents, we cannot succeed.

Every year I address more than 300 parents at our kindergarten registration sessions at Aquila and Peter Hobart Primary Centers. I offer them what can be the most exciting partnership of their lives: partnership with their children's schools. If they accept that offer, I can nearly guarantee their child's success throughout school. If they decline—if they believe that they can "deliver" any child to professional educators and "pick him up" educated and finished thirteen years later—then I predict a rocky road for that child.

Of course, we educators must do our part not only for each child but for the home-school partnership. But we can do only so much. To make a child successful in school, we need parents who engage in frequent communications with teachers, show daily interest in schoolwork, discuss values and school issues with children, help with homework, spend time in the classroom (even a few hours during the school year can make a difference for your own child and his or her classmates), and model all the joy of learning in their own lives.

The fact that you are reading this book suggests that I'm "preaching to the choir" about the importance of parent involvement. You want to give your children the positive experiences and supportive relationships that serve as a bedrock for future learning. But I challenge you to go further.

As I look at today's society and today's public schools, I must caution you that taking care of your own child is no longer enough. Even if your family is strong, the challenges facing other families are bound to affect yours.

I'm often asked, "Are the public schools working?" My answer is "Yes and no." Yes—in places where children come to school ready to learn, with parents who want to be partners. No—where failed family relationships, child abuse, a lack of love and encouragement have drained from children their enthusiasm, optimism, natural curiosity, and desire to learn.

If you want your own children to thrive, you must join with educators, business people, social service providers, and local governments to improve the lives of all children in your community. More than 12 million children in the U.S.—about one in five—are poor. Children are almost twice as likely to be poor as any other group of Americans, including the elderly. Each year about 350,000 children are born to mothers who are addicted to cocaine during pregnancy. About 40,000 children are born each year with alcohol-related birth defects. Twenty percent of America's preschool children have not been vaccinated against polio. About 20 percent of handicapped children could have been born healthy if their mothers had received just one physical examination in the first trimester of pregnancy. According to Dr. Harold Hodgkinson, "More than one-third of America's children are at risk of failure in school even before they enter the kindergarten door."

There's no use running away—from the inner city to the suburbs, or from the public school to a private school. The problems are everywhere, and even if you can escape from poverty or a high crime rate, even in the suburbs too few children are motivated to excel. Employers and teachers complain about the disappearance of the work ethic.

Schools—even the best schools, like those in St. Louis Park, Minnesota, where Anne Stokes is a staff member—simply do not have the talent, training skills, or resources for both a social mission and an educational mission. We simply cannot do both jobs.

Only with the commitment of the total community can we again put children first—all children. The total community must stand behind families, giving them the support they need to be their children's first and most important teachers.

We need a collaborative approach with schools, government, social services, businesses, civic organizations, and religious groups, each contributing what they do best, working in harmony toward common goals.

The Thinking Parent: Understanding and Guiding Your Child is a first step for growing as parents. Putting these suggestions and skills into practice gives positive, focused direction to your critical role as your child's first and most important educator. The next step is to reach beyond your own families and join hands with others in assuming responsibility for all of our children in all of our communities. Working together, I believe we can more than "make it." We can create a synergy that can change the world for children.

Carl A. Holmstrom, Ed.D.
Superintendent, St. Louis Park Public Schools, Minnesota

Preface

There's a rumble like a developing earthquake under the homes in our communities. If you listen in, you will hear the frustrated mutterings of thousands of parents.

"Are all children like that?"

"How do I get my child to do what he is told to do?"

"How does a working parent find time for 'quality time'?"

"My child doesn't care if she learns anything!"

"My kids are an embarrassment! They have no manners!"

The funny thing is that these are the mutterings of "good" parents in "good" homes. "Good" parents whose children have already resorted to violence and self-destructive or socially destructive activity are beyond these simple questions. But all "good" parents need reassurance, support, and suggestions. They want to avoid the truly terrible child behavior abyss in which many families are trapped today. They are looking for preventive measures and for ways to enhance family relationships.

The Thinking Parent: Understanding and Guiding Your Child is written for parents of elementary-age children, but it also contains material appropriate for parents of preschool children. Some parents feel that more material is written for ages one to five than for elementary ages. However, the principles of good child rearing that apply to very young children are the foundation of the principles that deal with older children. This book translates those early foundational principles and applies them to the kindergarten through the grade-six child. To the extent that the principles are basic, this book might be for any age.

What I propose and suggest in these pages is based on my experience as coordinator of an early childhood family education program in a public school and on the parent education newsletter that I have written for many years. A number of important topics are addressed that will interest parents of children from the early years before school through grade six. This is because it has been my experience that parents using the library at our parent education program are eager to find books addressing more than one topic. While there always are, and will be, families in need of answers to specific, often serious, problems, a very large percentage of them seem to have a more varied array of interests and want a broader based volume of help for their parenting concerns, that is, a general parenting book.

Many books on parenting the elementary child are part of a rather definite parenting "system," giving parents a step-by-step action plan. If you follow the directions, they will work for many people. The problem comes in all the variations that families bring to such systems. The personalities of both parents and children, the home environment, and all the external and internal pressures that are part of it affect the ability of a family to use a given system. Also, many systems relate to only one aspect of child rearing, such as discipline, communication, or self-esteem. I am not aware of as many general parenting books for the elementary age as seem to be available for infants, toddlers, and preschoolers.

If you take away the trappings of most systems, they begin at one point: think. This material tries to use a common sense approach that acknowledges the uniqueness of each parent and child and encourages parents to think through their own special solutions to child-rearing quandaries. The book doesn't offer a system or a "quick fix." Rather, it is based on the following assumptions:

• No one knows this child as well as this parent.

• The parent is an intelligent, searching person (or they wouldn't have bought this book).

• The parent is looking for a way to sort out the occasional chaos and frustration of parenting.

In short, *The Thinking Parent* assumes a parent who wants to "think about" what is going on with the child and develop a plan that works for her (his) own particular family.

Some of the chapters in this book offer a foundation for the parent's thoughts. Child development information is crucial if we are to understand why a child behaves in a particular way. We need to know where the child is coming from. Is this the way children of this age usually behave? Other chapters deal with character development and child management. These chapters end with an action summary, things the concerned parent should think about before acting. None of these are a system in themselves. They assume that the parent will think about the issues raised, decide whether the points are valid and how they apply to their own child, and then act on them in their own unique way. To the extent that thinking is a "system," I am perhaps guilty of creating still another one.

Parenting is hard work. Why do I care how successful parents are in the hard work of guiding their children? I care about children. Children grow into competent, self-actualized individuals in families. I also strongly believe that a major component of a balanced federal budget is a healthy society in which fewer dollars are needed to heal areas of dysfunction. Since the family is the foundational institution in our society, efforts to prevent family dysfunction can ultimately save our nation billions of dollars.

I maintain that America's role in the world is based on

the competence of individuals whose character, motivation, and skill have been nurtured in those basic family institutions. Getting to that point requires a long, slow, healing process. We may not always be able to see how our own families are related to that vast vision; we may get lost in the crowd. But be assured that what parents do today is, and always will be, of Earth-shaping importance!

Dedication

To Ken, whose constant support made this possible,
and to Alan, Randy, Brad, and Hap,
whom we are proud to love and who made us think.

Contents

FOREWORD ... v

PREFACE ... x

INTRODUCTION ... 1
The Perfect Parenting Myth

1 A LOOK AT DEVELOPMENT ... 6
"Is This My Child?"

2 AN INTRODUCTION TO SELF-ESTEEM ... 17
"Can I Like Me?"

3 MORAL DEVELOPMENT ... 32
"What Is Right and What Is Wrong?"

4 DEVELOPING INTERNAL CONTROL ... 50
"Who's in Charge Here?"

5 COMMON COURTESY ... 57
Simple—But Uncommon—Words Today

6 YOUR CHILD AND WORK ... 67
The Hard Work of Developing Helpful Children

7 FAMILY RITUALS AND TRADITIONS ... 76
Building Memories and Cementing Values

8 THE ART OF ASKING QUESTIONS   83
   "Talk To Me! I'll Listen!"

9 DISCIPLINE AND PUNISHMENT   90
   "What Do I Expect?"

10 TAKING TIME   104
   Is It Quality Time or Everydailyness?

11 YOUR PARENTING STYLE   110
   "What Kind of Parent Am I?"

12 MOTIVATION TO LEARN   122
   "My Kid Doesn't Want to Learn!"

13 BEGINNING A NEW SCHOOL YEAR   129
   Resolutions

Introduction

The Perfect Parenting Myth

Once upon a time in a faraway land, a family decided to raise a perfect child. To do this, they reasoned (quite logically) they would have to be perfect parents.

With enthusiasm they tackled terrible twoness, bedtime battles, temper tantrums, learning to share, and following the rules. This perfect child was raised to have a sweet and unselfish temperament, to always make his bed in the morning, to do his chores without being asked, to come when called, to respond politely, to adore his sister, to sit quietly in his house of worship, to love shopping trips and long car rides and hours in the doctor's waiting room, and above all else, to adore going to school. In fact, he was always ready for the school bus ahead of time with his lunch (which he had packed himself, of course) and all of his homework, clean gym clothes (washed by himself, of course), and library books.

And so it was, in this faraway land, that this perfect child began to meet the world. The perfect parents of the perfect child waited expectantly for the adulation that would come as the world discovered that they did indeed have the formula for producing perfection.

It was with great distress that they began to discover that all was not well.

Their *per*fect *ch*ild (whom we shall call Perch) was completely miserable. The other children would not share and he didn't know what to do. They didn't respond to his perfect responses. The teachers sent home notes: "Perch is a perfect doormat." After all, Perch was really so very nice that anything that wasn't nice left him nonplussed. Other children resented this shining example. Perch has his homework done. Perch knows the answers. Perch doesn't forget his gym clothes. And how could anyone deal with a child who didn't know who the Teenage Mutant Ninja Turtles were?

"Perch is a fish! Perch is a fish!" the children taunted. And indeed he *was* a fish out of water. It was with dismay that these perfect parents began to display all of the symptoms of stress. They slept and ate poorly. They thought they might be getting ulcers. They had muscle cramps and panic attacks. Their psychiatrist finally pinpointed it as PPS (Perfect Parent Syndrome). It was bad enough that they were hypercritical of themselves, but when Perch would remind them to pick up their dirty socks and to stop discussions that had hardly yet become arguments, they felt stifled and guilty.

There was only one solution. They must all learn to relax and live a little. Retraining Perch to be *imp*erfect (known later as Imp) was just as difficult as training him to be perfect. Years later, however, his parents agreed that it had been worth the effort. Learning to live with Perch had been terrible. Imp was indeed a human being!

The obvious but important moral of this fable is that no one is perfect. We are all indeed very human. We live in an imperfect world in which our children must use their most creative skills to flourish and grow well. Perfect children might very well find an imperfect world a difficult place to live. And keeping up the standards of perfection would produce unbelievable levels of stress. Instead, let's look at what constitutes a "perfectly good parent."

What Does the Good Parent Do?
1. The good parent always loves the child, but not necessarily all of the child's behavior. The good parent is able to separate love for the child from feelings about the child's behavior. This means that at times when you'd like to disown your child, your deepest self knows that this is "your own very special loved one."

2. The good parent knows that because the child is loved he (she) needs and wants discipline and limits. Good parents anticipate problems and set limits beforehand. When a situation arises, they *act* and act right away. Warnings about "how many minutes until_____" are necessary and a sign of respect. However, counting to 10 when the child fails to obey is a wishy-washy postponing of the consequences.

3. The good parent is consistent but not rigid. Sometimes good reasoning tells us to be flexible. But flexibility is not being wishy-washy. It means changing things for a good reason. The good parent is clear. Words like "nice" and "be good" are defined by telling the child exactly what actions are expected. "I expect you to sit in the car without hitting your brother!"

4. The good parent sometimes makes mistakes. Apologizing for a mistake is perfectly appropriate. It is a good example for the child to follow. Don't you want your child to be able to say, "I was wrong but I'll do better!"? What if the child assumes the parent is always perfect? Wouldn't that be a stressful example to live up to? How could such a child ever get to the point of admitting to mistakes and learning from them?

5. The good parent communicates with the child and with the other parent (whether or not you live together).

Communication is a key to good family relations. This means both talking and listening. Communication is not demanding, lecturing, yelling, and blaming. It does mean that you express feelings honestly, listen to the feelings of others, ask for ideas, negotiate, plan, compromise, provide information, and problem solve.

6. *The good parent finds ways to spend time with the child.* The time spent may be what Burton White calls "parenting on the fly." This means taking the minutes while you are preparing the meal to carry on conversations and find out about the day, using the time in the car for verbal games, or making up stories, cleaning house together, and making chores a family activity. The myth of quality time seems to suggest that it can make up for all those very daily minutes when the family members need to have the support of each other and feel that each one cares. Don't forget those many minutes. Use them. They are the most important minutes of all!

7. *Perhaps most important, the good parent is realistic:* basing expectations for self and child on some real understandings of each family member as a person:
- What can be expected of each?
- How much stress is too much for each?
- What are the interests of each?
- What are the needs of each?
- How can each learn from rough times as well as successes?

What the Good Parent Is Not

1. *The good parent is not a magician.* There is no wonder formula for raising children. What works one time will fail miserably the next. Just as we get the hang of it, our child will erupt into a new stage and all the rules will change.

2. *The good parent does not expect to know it all.* Common sense is essential but sometimes not enough. It does help to

get expert knowledge on child development and behavior. It does help to get the teacher's input.

3. *The good parent is not a paragon of virtuous patience.* Parents are sometimes angry enough to wonder why anyone ever has children, because children do not always behave in lovable ways. At such times we may "lose" it. No matter how many times the "correct" responses have been practiced, they won't always be on the tip of the tongue.

4. *The good parent is not necessarily a perfect housekeeper or gourmet cook.* There are many reasons for having to admit that you can't provide your own special decadent brownies for the class party. Expense, lack of time, and lack of cooking skill may all enter in. All parents are busy, some working outside the home, some finding the demands of parenting exhausting, and others putting in long hours volunteering. Accept the fact that you are busy. Buy the doggoned cookies; spend only what you can afford.

So you haven't time to clean behind the refrigerator every week. I have dust balls older than my grandfather! My kids never noticed (they weren't perfect either) and certainly the band that rehearsed in our basement never noticed. I often felt they did me a service by vibrating the dirt away! Forget the guilt! That's the way things are!

5. *The good parent does not feel that all personal interests and individuality must be sacrificed because of the family.* Let your child see that you are a unique individual with interests of your own, with respect for yourself and respect for your own competence. Your child will learn to feel that way, too, seeing that this is the way personhood is defined in your family.

Parenting is exhausting! Don't try to be perfect!

But do consider parenting as the most important thing you have ever done!

1

A Look at Development

"Is This My Child?"

When our youngest son was in sixth grade, his teacher called to invite us to a school assembly. Hap was getting an award. "Our son? The one who hasn't let us cut his hair for two months? The one who has worn the same sun visor both in and out of school (and into the shower and then to bed) for three months? The one who screams when we want to wash the T-shirt that he has worn for fully four months because it is decorated with his friends' signatures? Our son?"

Parents often feel that they don't know their elementary-age child because these are the years when the child shuts out the adult and joins the society of children. It's a time when the child looks to other children as the authority for action: "But, Dad, I have to do it! All the other kids are!"

This chapter is a brief overview of development for children ages kindergarten through grade six. Children rarely fit a developmental profile perfectly, but usually the descriptions provide a way for parents to understand the joys and concerns they feel about their children. It helps to know that "kids are like that!" Let's begin with the years from five to seven.

Ages Five to Seven: Social-Emotional Development

During this period your child takes a giant step both socially and intellectually. This is the time when a child makes great social strides in discovering the people and relationships in the world outside the home. Your child's great social changes are triggered by going to school:
- Peers become important.
- He (she) puts trust in another adult, the teacher.
- She (he) may see these other people for more hours daily than they see your family.

Before children reach these "school years" there has usually been an adult nearby to prompt them to "be nice" to each other. Adults help younger children put themselves in another's shoes and see things from another's perspective. We don't expect the preschool child to show understanding and empathy without an adult present as prompter. How many times did you admonish your preschooler: "Cheryl is unhappy because you took her toy away!" "Charles, help Jerry with that box!"? Now that you aren't there all the time, will your child still think about these things?

The child at five, six, or seven is still learning what it means to have a friend. The rules for making friends aren't developed. They may:
- decide on friends simply by asking a child to be a friend and then telling the same child that they don't want to be friends any more
- choose friends on the basis of the toys or abilities they possess
- try to buy friends with presents

- bargain for friends with promises to invite them to their parties
- beat up the other child just to get the child's attention.

Suddenly the child is thrust into a room with 25 "new friends." Not only must he (she) get along with these children, but also learn new academic concepts in their presence. The child is open to public criticism for failure and public approval for success.

Until the child gets the new social rules straight, there may be more showing off and less cooperation than exhibited at five. And it isn't until well beyond the five-to-seven shift that the child can accurately understand some of the more complicated feelings of another child—feelings more complicated than happiness or sadness.

Is it any wonder, then, that the child in this period shows extremes of behavior—from loving to hostile; from joy to anger? The six year old, particularly, may add to these swings in behavior the inability to make a decision. The child wavers between chocolate and vanilla ice cream, blue or red socks, or any other simple choice.

During this period your child becomes more interested in the sex of playmates. Sexually stereotyped play may be evident. Even today, when there is less differentiation between "boy toys" and "girl toys," children may segregate their own play. However, there is a fascination with sexual topics and with anatomy and marriage.

Children in this early elementary age may have a mania for certain activities. They will ride bikes daily with neighborhood children, or play a favorite game repeatedly. They find security in this repetitive activity with the same group of friends. These well-worn and familiar games provide occasions when the emphasis can be on learning to be with others rather than on having to think about game rules. The chosen activity has long since become acceptable and the rules have been memorized by playing the game over and over. Some young children want to change the rules as they go along so that they can win. This fits in with the fact that, developmentally, they are still unable to see the game from someone else's perspective. They don't yet see that built into the nature of playing a game is the challenge of sometimes winning and sometimes losing. They can be terrible "losers." Depending on their social "status," children who don't follow the rules exactly are sometimes ostracized. This can make game-playing a stormy activity. Ritualistic views of the rules are probably helpful during this stage.

Five to eight year olds can be creative in their dramatic play. They develop involved scenarios to fit either their own stories or the stories of favorite television characters. Props, conversation, sound effects, and some idea of a beginning and an ending are part of their pretending.

Rituals and chants become important as the child develops in a social group. Like repetitive games, the fun of a chant is that it's a social activity. Once the chant is learned, the child can concentrate on the social aspects. It doesn't matter whether it makes sense. "Its raining, it's pouring..." "Ladybug, ladybug, fly away home..." "Teddy bear, teddy bear, turn around..." are examples of this.

Parents are still important at this stage because the child has by now internalized the rules learned at home. When the standards or rules are broken, she (he) feels guilty, even when the parent may have no way of finding out. Therefore, the child tries hard to please a parent. Because ideas of right and wrong are very simple and inflexible at this stage, the child is fearful that being "bad" will cause the loss of the parent's love. Add to this fear the fact that the child is unsure of friends at a time when love and a sense of being worthwhile are desperately needed. His (her) frequent questions might include:

- "Is this all right?"
- "Will you be here?"

Ages Five to Seven: Intellectual Development

During this period there are biological changes that explain some of the changes we see in a child's thinking and behavior. The neurons in the brain, the connections between nerve cells, and the myelin sheath or "insulation" covering the nerves are all still in the process of development. The children have learned so much and are now in school, so we tend to forget that "they aren't done yet." Just as electricity can short-circuit in a poorly insulated electric cord, so messages travel more accurately and faster on completed, fully myelinated nerve pathways. Five-to-seven children still have a way to go! Though growing, the memory still is not great and the logic systems are still quite simple.

During this period the child "shifts" to being able to count with the eyes, store the information in the head, and think about it. Preschool children may not be able to think back to where they left their mittens without actually retracing their steps. They need actual objects to touch and manipulate when thinking through a problem. In order to count, the younger child has to touch each object. Between five and seven we see the child's increasing ability to work abstractly.

At first the child uses very simple rules when thinking through a problem, usually just one at a time. Consider this problem: in this row of circles, find the largest circle. To solve this problem the child uses just one rule, the rule of "size." By age seven the child can work with several rules. For example: In this row of many shapes, find the largest circle. Mark it with an X.

At home this means it is easier to give the child directions for chores. You can mention several steps at once. You can expect the child to do simple, logical reasoning. You can expect the child to *begin* to be able to figure out that some process or rule used in another situation might also work in the one at hand. For example, if the wet glass will leave a water mark on the finish of the coffee table, it may leave a ring on the dresser as well. Or, if you should hang up dish towels, you should also hang up bath towels.

In the early elementary years, it is wise to remember that these changes are new to your child. His (her) reasoning still must do a lot of growing. For example, your child has just come home from hockey and left his bike in the middle of the drive. You may want to shout, "I told you to put your bike away when you come home from school! What is wrong with your head?" But your child may not yet have matured enough to connect the "coming home from school" rule to all the other situations when coming home with a bike. Until the child's mind becomes completely logical, you may need to spell it out. During these years you will be continually meeting surprises whenever growth takes place and the child makes an unexpected automatic connection.

Because of the dawning of this ability to think abstractly, the five, six, and seven year olds begin to create learning strategies. Prior to this time, children have difficulty working things out in their heads. Toward the end of this period, some children can make their own flash cards, plan a poster-making assignment, or figure out what books to read to fulfill an assignment.

The ability to reason means that children can examine cause and effect. The consequences in a discipline situation can now be understood. If I do *this*, then *that* will happen. However, in helping a child reason things out, keep in mind that the curious and imaginative five-to-seven will make up a reason or a consequence (logical or wild) if there isn't a logical one given:

- "The teacher said I didn't have to do it!"

- "I couldn't do it because Sara would be mad and get me all dirty!"

Children develop as "whole persons." It is easy to see how their social and moral development, mentioned earlier, is connected to the intellectual development we have just described. Since the parent is still very important to the young elementary age child, the parent's rules will be very important too. It matters, then, that parents link the newly developing understanding of consequences and logic to the rules they establish.

Ages Eight to Twelve: Social-Emotional Development

The elementary school years are the time for taking little bites out of parent and teacher authority. As children grow, they find that the rules in the home were made by Mom and Dad, not by some mystical force. The rules can be broken. Reading by flashlight after "lights out," tearing up a homework paper, or sneaking cookies are all ways of learning that parents are not all-powerful. It takes great calm to firmly enforce the family rules when you feel your parental authority is being challenged. Keep in perspective the fact that this is a normal process of experimentation. Probably the child is more concerned with maintaining status with friends than with bucking parental power. In the world of the child's fleeting emotions, it is really reassuring to him (her) to have parents and teachers who can enforce the rules and bring order to the chaos.

During these years, as abstract thinking continues to develop, the child stops thinking out loud, reads silently, and begins building memories. Most people have very limited preschool memories. Memories begin to build as the child becomes old enough to attend elementary school. Part of this is because of a spurt in brain development; part of it is due to the normal awakening to a broader world. As the child's ability to plan and think ahead becomes more complex, learning skills become more deliberate strategies. Physical growth slows until puberty, perhaps to allow for the energies needed for social, emotional, and mental growth.

In this newly social world, eight to twelve year olds are seen everywhere they can manage to go: the mall, the corner store, sports events, in woods, by ponds, at playgrounds, at parades, garage sales, whatever. Nicknames are developed that fit the gang view of the child: Skinny, Big Joe, Twitch. Somehow most of these are not seen as derogatory if the child is socially accepted.

Because they still cannot totally understand another's point of view, the conversations of eight to ten year olds may be one-sided. They jabber away with each other but don't really say much:

"Did you see that girl over there?" (whispered with great exaggeration).
"Which one?"
"That one!"
"Oh!"
"She's got on that pretty color of blue!"
"Yeah! (giggle, whisper) I see her."

The growing children of middle years still love rituals. Although the ritual still doesn't have to make any sense, they may increasingly create their own chants to fit their own culture or daily events. The Rap craze, for example, may fit the child's interest in contemporary rhythm and jargon. Along with the enjoyment of the rhythm is the security of being part of the chanting group and the recognition and satisfaction that they know all the words.

In the later elementary years, children learn to adapt game rules to suit themselves. They can figure a more complex way to win, a new route to the prize, a more complicated way to play tag, or a new way to score a point. When they were younger the rules of games were viewed ritualistically and certain games were played obsessively. There was no praise or acceptance if they thought up a new twist to the rules.

Although creativity and abstract thinking allow the eight to twelve year old to let go of a ritualistic need for game rules that never change, they still have a need for ritual. Ritual, for example, is part of their desire and need to make collections. Boxes and drawers of almost anything can be regarded as a collection, which takes on ritual and magical qualities to the child. Ritual is also part of the obsessive need to wear the same clothes or become attached to a certain routine.

The child's play between the ages of eight and twelve progresses from unorganized group play with lots of self-testing, wild running and chasing to stronger individual interests in either organized sports, hobbies, or complicated table games. They may make up quite sophisticated games or add to the games they already know, and work at complex crafts or produce imaginative plays. By age ten to twelve the onset of puberty makes the child very aware of bodily changes. Clumsiness or gawkiness may be a problem if there is rapid growth. In this stage, however, most children, both boys and girls, delight in all kinds of physical activity. Team sports become important because they involve both social activity and a testing of individual skill. Since children twelve and under thrive on attention, these middle years are the perfect show-off period. They need an audience, partly because they are still unable to step outside themselves in order to examine their own performance; they need an audience to do this for them.

Children in the early elementary years may have unrealistic ideas about what they can actually do. However, nine year olds are able to make realistic plans and carry out some of them. They respond to praise and want to achieve. Up to now, their moral sense included ideas of fair play, but usually only when it was of benefit to themselves. This older elementary child may now have a concern to be considered "good." It's easy, though, for this to get mixed up with peer pressure: what the gang considers "good." This stage can be helpful, however, when combined with positive adult approval and what they learn about good motives. However, it is still important for them to talk about what is "fair."

Because of the changes in social understanding, peer pressure to conform becomes more pronounced. To be accepted as a friend by another child requires being at one's best all the time. Parents and teachers must accept the child *as is*, but friends are earned. The trust exhibited in these relationships is usually very strong. It develops first as a two-way cooperation: "I'll help you if you'll help me." By age ten to twelve, friendships are mutually shared relationships where friends tell each other everything and are intimate and exclusive. They really dislike six to nine year olds, but enjoy preschool children. And, of course, their interest in the other sex grows.

During the last of the elementary years, the physical changes in girls are dramatic. Because many enter puberty during this time, their social behavior is also quite different from boys. Communication between the sexes is limited, but they are very aware of each other sexually.

Ages Eight to Twelve: Intellectual Development

Children between ages eight and twelve are learning new skills rapidly and with a true perfectionism. They expect to be instantly good at everything they attempt, but their frustrations are real and frequent. They often say, "I'm no good at that!" "I can't do anything right!" or, as a cover-up, "That's boring!"

Children are apt to be more well-balanced at eight, ten,

and twelve than at the odd-numbered years. This means that the frustrations experienced are handled better in the "even" years, which are good times to help them learn to see things from another's perspective. It is also a good time to be teaching self-evaluation skills.

Older elementary children can use symbols and abstract thinking well enough to develop codes, secret writing, and new game rules. They can think of the future and the distant past and thus think of history. While plans may still be a bit unrealistic, these intellectual skills enhance their ability to develop and carry out some worthwhile ideas. During this period they grow toward the ability to solve problems by testing hypotheses and thinking out consequences. They use fewer trial-and-error approaches.

One odd quirk during this time is a sort of all-or-nothing-at-all thinking. If they discover that parents are less than perfect and don't know *everything*, then they may well decide that parents, therefore, don't know *anything*. This "cognitive conceit" leads children to be more sure of abilities than they should be and sometimes results in efforts to do things they shouldn't.

Understanding where your child is developmentally may help in creating harmony at home. Knowledge is often the basis for wisdom, but knowledge also goes hand-in-hand with common sense.

2

AN INTRODUCTION TO SELF-ESTEEM

"Can I Like Me?"

I hate anyone who doesn't have to cover her knees. The next-door neighbor doesn't have to cover anything. I, on the other hand, cover the windows. It isn't what my husband can see that worries me; it's a fear that *she* can see *me*. It's the mortal blow to my self-esteem. I'm definitely not a size 8.

I often attend self-esteem workshops related to parent education. (Self-esteem workshops have very high opinions of themselves. The outcomes are never stated half way! Instead they proclaim, "At this workshop you will...!") At one such workshop, the director was adamant: "If you learned anything today, you'll wear this button out on the street. I *dare* you to wear it to the store!" I got as far as my car. Then I took it off; I hadn't learned enough. The button said: I LIKE ME!

How strange that we'll wear all sorts of other labels: T-shirts with arrows labeling the expected new baby, political messages, environmental decrees, even our ages. We also will monogram everything. It makes things look expensive! We mark things to make them uniquely our own. We're proud of our possessions. Yet, our most precious possession is one we are not at all sure we are proud of, not at all sure we want to label and hold up for the eyes of the world. Our most precious possession is our sense of self, our image of who we are, and our judgment of whether that image is good or bad.

The self-image, self concept, or perception of self is the way we define ourselves. Self-esteem is a judgment about the worth of that self-concept. It can be positive or negative.

To feel secure, confident, and ready to cope, children need a high self-esteem. To live with vigor and courage, children must know who they are and what they can do. Self-esteem is vital. Did you know that, for a child, a positive self-concept and self-esteem may be more important for school achievement than the IQ level? Often when a teacher or parent treats a child like an achiever, the child will be an achiever regardless of aptitude test scores. The child accomplishes what he or she believes to be accomplishable. Determination and self-confidence are of prime importance. We become what we believe ourselves to be.

The self-concept is made of at least two parts:
- the reflected view of ourselves seen in the mirror of family, teachers, and friends
- the self-appraisals we form as we examine ourselves in action, examine our behavior and its consequences.

These two parts of the self-concept are interlocked in ways that are sometimes confusing. Where does this strong view of the self come from?

Comparisons and Relationships
1. Our self-esteem is built through our relationships with people. It also can be destroyed by poor relationships. We decide

whether we are good or bad at something by looking at those around us. We learn about ourselves from looking at others in our immediate family, extended family, neighborhood, and community.

For me, the final blow to the "I hate to cook" generation came when I had to shatter my children's illusions about my cooking! They had always come willingly to the table. My satisfaction at having put enough food on the table for four teen-aged boys was always short-lived because of their vacuum-cleaner approach to eating. The blow came because my sons bragged to the church youth group about my spaghetti sauce. The group wanted the recipe for a fund-raiser dinner. How could I tell this gang that my famous, unique, delectable sauce came out of a foil packet? I was caught in the same scam as the lady in the Rice Krispie bar ad on television! I wondered what her kids would do to her if they found out. I knew I was a poor cook! My best friend belonged to a gourmet club!

You may consider yourself very "unhandy" because you have never built or fixed anything very significant. You may feel useless in comparison to a neighbor who spends several days a week volunteering at a school. Your daughter may consider herself ugly because she doesn't have curly hair like a popular classmate's. Or your son may consider himself a poor artist because his admired friend draws great jets. Or perhaps it's a feeling of stupidity because others are better at reading.

2. *In order to make sense of the images of ourselves that we see reflected in relationships with others, we need to take an analytic perspective.* We need to evaluate what we see about ourselves. For example, my husband and I learned to ski when we were 50. We soon grew dissatisfied with Minnesota's "bumps" and developed a taste for Colorado mountains. There's nothing beautiful about our style. It's based quite logically on standing up at all costs. We could feel really em-

barrassed at our skill level, but instead we look around at the young hotshots on the intermediate slopes and note that we're among the oldest skiers there. And we're having fun. Our attitude is relational. We can evaluate our feelings about ourselves as skiers when we take all the issues into account: our age, when we learned, our enjoyment.

Perhaps you aren't a gourmet cook, but your family likes what you cook. You may consider yourself "unhandy" until half the neighborhood comes over to admire the garden shed you just built. Or perhaps you are a handyman klutz, but you are the one everyone turns to for advice at income tax time. Maybe your neighbor is at school more than you are, but then you realize that this neighbor considers you a saint for babysitting her preschool child so that she is free to volunteer.

Dorothy Corkille Briggs writes that the process of learning about the self is very much like looking in a series of psychological mirrors. Everywhere we go, the world holds up a mirror. We catch glimpses of ourselves in these varied mirrors of life. Sometimes we like the reflection we see; sometimes we don't. But we learn a great deal about ourselves from analyzing the reflections.

- The teacher liked my picture. I must be a good artist!
- The neighbors liked my cake. I must be a good baker!
- The neighbors didn't like my cake. It was still a good cake. Not everyone likes coconut.
- The boss liked my presentation. I must be a valuable employee!
- I thought I did well, even if they didn't think so. Look at the effect this plan had on the group!

Family Relationships

The first relationships are family relationships. Parents, of course, have the first and most far-reaching influence on the child's self-concept and self-esteem. Learning who I am, what I can do, and how much I am valued begins at birth and develops realistically step-by-step throughout life. The child's feelings about himself or herself are *learned* just as the child learns to recognize parents, to grasp objects, to know where the hand ends and the rattle begins. If the child is loved, if parents respond to the child's cries, if the child feels secure and comfortable, the first feelings of worth can germinate.

The family provides for children the first mirrors in which they can view themselves. Family members are always telling children in words and action what they think of them and who they are. When the feedback says "You are good, nice-looking, or intelligent," children believe it. Conversely, when children receive negative reflections from the family mirror, they assume the reflections are true.

Often the reflections we offer to a child have to do with behavior in situations where the child must be punished. Discipline and self-esteem go hand in hand. For example, the child may come to feel:

- "If Mom says I am bad, I must be bad!"
- Even worse: "If they think I'm bad, I may as well act that way!"

In the chapter on moral development I note that a child judges an act on the basis of the kind of punishment it brings. When we try to manage children's behavior, it's easy to destroy their feeling that they are worthy to be loved. Often, too, the reflections we offer children have to do with success at school.

- "Boy, you're really dumb!"
- "Why can't you be smart like your brother?"
- "You never get anything right!"

Competence and ability are linked with the picture that children have of themselves. Children hearing these statements soon *believe* themselves to be incompetent and they *act* incompetently. The tools for viewing the self that are developed in the home are then taken out into the world where the views of peers and teachers become part of the picture the child has created of himself or herself. What emerges is a self that is a social product.

We want our children to feel good about themselves. We want them to achieve what is worthwhile because they have a deeply rooted feeling that they are worthy and capable. Our job becomes more difficult because we cannot control a great deal of what happens to our children once they begin doing things outside the home. If we feel we are having a hard time keeping the home picture positive, we have even less influence over what happens outside the home.

What can a parent do to help a child develop a strong, healthy self-concept?

1. *Look at your own self-concept.* Do you feel good about yourself? Do you like yourself? Why? As parents, we are mirrors reflecting back the child's self-picture. Yet, our feelings about ourselves cloud the image our mirrors reflect for our children. Research shows that parents with fuzzy self-concepts and low self-esteem raise children with poor self-concepts and low self-esteem. Start working on your child's self-esteem by working on your own.

Many of us were brought up to be humble, modest. We don't believe in "tooting our own horn" or saying "I like myself!" But even if we don't say it, if our lives don't reflect some self-confidence and satisfaction with ourselves, our children will never grow to learn what that feeling is or might be.

2. *Love your children unconditionally.* Let your children know that you love them *no matter what*, regardless of accomplishments. It is your free gift to the child just for being born. It is expressed when you say things such as:

- "I'm glad you're our daughter!"

- "We like going to hockey games with you!"
- "It's good to be a family, and for you to be part of it!"

There will be times when both you and your children know that they aren't much fun to have around. Realize that that is normal.

3. *Encourage your children.* Offer lots of specific encouragement sprinkled with very limited amounts of praise. Encouragement means mentioning specific *behaviors* that you like, instead of praising the child's *character*. For example, an encouraging comment might be: "I like the way you hung up your clothes!" A comment that praises character might be: "You're a good boy!" When you comment with such broad and general praise of a child's character, he (she) may not know exactly what pleased you.

Offer encouragement by saying, "The teacher was really pleased when you solved this math problem!" This helps the child evaluate and understand the components of a good paper. Global praise might be, "I see you were very smart today!" This does nothing to help the child see exactly what has pleased the teacher.

Sometimes it's appropriate to discuss character. Sometimes (and maybe more often) it's appropriate to give the child the tools to evaluate his (her) work and behavior by being very specific.

4. *Avoid labeling and name-calling* when you must punish. As I've already mentioned, focus on the behavior, not the character of the child—even when you're sure the child can't be a member of your well-mannered family and was probably beamed down from outer space. Describe *specific* behavior.

Instead of saying "You're bad!" say, "You forgot the rule about coming straight home from school. You didn't get home until 4:00 and I was worried!" When you say, "You are bad! " you are being a mirror that shows the child an image of self as bad. Children often live up to the images we project, the labels we give them. Try a specific, positive statement. (Being a "good girl" may be too much to live up to. After all, what does it mean to be "good"?) Here are two examples:

- "You are such a fine dish-dryer" is specific and encourages the child to try again.
- "You are so kind to your dog" is a behavior a child can pinpoint and repeat.

5. *Set realistic goals for your child and with your child.* Break big jobs up into small, easily accomplished steps. It's so much easier to keep at a job when there are strings of small triumphs along the way. Planning jobs together often helps both parent and child in understanding what is possible, how to do it, and what to expect. Take time to train your child in the skills needed to accomplish a task. Help your child to feel like a success at home and school. Acknowledge willingness and effort.

6. *Affirm your child's efforts to work and think for self and allow for failure when it comes.* Helping your child figure out what went wrong, what to change, and what to do next affirms your faith in his (her) basic ability in spite of the setback. Failure does not mean that we are inadequate people; it only means that our plan of attack, our behavior, was inadequate. No one can be perfect. If failure is not allowed, if it is punished or ridiculed, the child might either set unattainable goals for perfection or give up altogether. Either way is stressful and damaging.

7. *Learn to guide and facilitate instead of always directing or dictating.* Your child can learn that you have confidence in his (her) own ability to solve problems. Of course, you are always there to be sure that solutions are wise. This is *not* the time to lock yourself in the bathroom! Ask, "What would you like me to do to help you?"

8. *Keep a "stroke" count.* How many times have you made positive, encouraging statements today? How many times

have you been critical or negative? If the negatives outweigh the positives, you may need to work harder at boosting your child's self-esteem.

Children need to know that you approve of them and love them. They do not need to have you gush a lot of insincere praise. Children can understand very well when a reward is earned and also when they have missed the mark.

The Child's View of Self

There are always children who seem to feel terrible about themselves, no matter how many times you tell them they are lovable and capable. They think they are ugly when they are beautiful, fat when they are really thin, stupid when they are smart. It's hard to tell where a young child gets such ideas if they come from a warm and loving family. But occasionally, in such cases, it is because the parents don't feel good about themselves either. This doesn't need to be expressed in words; children simply sense it from years of watching how parents act. Recall the importance of the parent's own self-concept. According to Dorothy Briggs, "You nourish from overflow, not from emptiness!" If you want your children to feel confident, first look at yourself.

I have already discussed the self as a social-relational creation. We judge who we are and how good we are at various activities by comparing ourselves to others. You may consider your child to be bright, but if your child knows that there are three other children who consistently score higher in math, she may not think so highly of her ability. The family mirror may be reflecting a very positive image but the child sees someone else who is better and finds it discouraging. Remember, the two parts of the self-concept are interlocked in confusing ways.

Unfortunately, in such instances, it isn't what the parent tells the child that counts. The thing that affects the child's self-concept is the way the child sees himself (herself) in relation to others. Children often seem to confuse their perceptions. Their stories are full of misconceptions and misinterpretations. They haven't learned to analyze their perceptions and get them into perspective. One wise parent told his child's teacher, "I won't believe half of what I hear about school if you will only believe half of what you hear about our home." Children may even be very sure that no one loves them, in spite of some real work on your part to help them feel cherished. Saying you love them will not automatically translate into a good self-concept with a feeling of being loved. *Being* loved and *feeling* loved are unfortunately not the same. Being successful and feeling successful are also not the same.

These ideas might help children to feel good about themselves:

1. Listen carefully. Children express their feelings in many ways. Listening may mean sorting out some inner meanings and "between-the-lines" messages.

2. Watch carefully. Not all feelings are expressed in words; some are expressed through a child's behavior. A sudden change in behavior patterns may be a clue that the child has new worries, new concerns about self, new relationship problems. Inner tensions are acted out in many ways.

3. Don't deny that the child has negative feelings. Try to be non-judgmental. Don't squelch the child's expression of feelings and concerns by saying:

- "No, you don't want that!"
- "You know that's a silly idea!"
- "Why would you think such a dumb thing?"

Acknowledge the child's feelings, but do not pity. The "Oh, you poor thing!" approach is just another way of saying that a child is small, pitiable, and powerless. The child has a right to have feelings. Focus on the feelings: "You really feel hurt about the way Susie treated you!" Ask the child what she (he) is going to do about a situation instead of automatically telling her (him) what to do. Be more concerned about what a child intends to *do* about the feelings than about the fact that the child is *having* those feelings. Ask the child why she (he) feels this way.

4. *Help the child to think through any difficult emotional statements or inappropriate actions.*
- "How would you feel if that really happened?"
- "Why does that matter to you?"
- "Is that more important than....?"

5. *Don't punish or deliver lectures about feelings.* We want children to know that everyone has feelings. They need help in analyzing whether the feelings are appropriate. They need to *actively* think through the issues, *not passively* listen.

6. *Teach creative self-evaluation.* Help your child to learn to evaluate his (her) efforts honestly, constructively, and creatively. Creative evaluation always includes looking at ways to do something differently the next time and it always ends with an emphasis on the good points.

7. *Look at the total picture of the child and help the child to do so too.* Don't joke too much. She (he) may need more than these flip comments:
- "So you have braces! Think of how much sparkle the camera flash gives to your smile!"
- "Don't worry. You'll have a shape someday. Just be glad you can wear Mom's pink sweater!"

Talk more with the child about his (her) concerns.

We are composites of our many views of our many relationships and experiences. Help children to put these together without giving too much weight to a single trait or experience. Remember the previous suggestions as you work this through.

Values and Self-Concept

Sometimes our evaluations of our relationships are made on

the basis of our values. Looking again at our gourmet cook, if unusual food and meal preparation is very important in your house, the discovery that you have a neighbor whose gourmet cooking puts you to shame may be an especially hard blow to the ego. But if your feelings concerning food call for simple, healthful meals, your ego won't be damaged much by the fancy meals next door. You wouldn't want such food, so you don't really care.

The child who feels stupid in math may feel that way because parents have said over and over that math is of vital importance. Knowing how important math is makes the child painfully aware of his or her class standing. Parents have made the comparisons very clear and may perhaps have overestimated the value of math in the total picture. In this instance, the math does have to be learned, but parents may find a middle ground between having a math whiz and acceptable mastery. And, sometimes, if the child feels successful in another subject, there is a dribble-down effect that helps the weaker subjects along.

The child whose parent spends hours watching sports and signs him (her) up for every team, whether or not the child wants it, is sending the child a message about the value of sports. Even if the parent says it doesn't matter if the child is a star, the child feels that it is important to be a star in order to please the parent.

Our four boys are Eagle Scouts. Grandpa was a Boy Scout leader or advisor for over 40 years. We told each boy that he could choose whether to pursue the Eagle award. When the fourth son came along, we magnanimously told him that we weren't going to pressure him to finish. He looked at us in exasperation and responded, "You don't really think I have any choice, do you?" It was obvious that we valued Scouting; his brothers were Eagle Scouts; his grandfather was a leader. He knew he couldn't live with a negative decision.

An Introduction to Self-Esteem

How can we help our children handle the comparisons when they feel they are in competition with others? Here are just a few ideas:

1. *Analyze what is important.* Carefully analyze what is important to you and what is important to your children.
   - Are they the same things? If not, why not?
   - Is education important? Is it just important to you—or to your child also? Why?
   - Are curly hair or artistic ability important? Are they important to you or just to your child? Why?

If, for example, you think curly hair is unimportant, it won't help to just tell your child it's silly. It may help to find pictures of admired movie stars, athletes, friends of your child whose hair styles don't depend on curls. It may also help to spend some time discussing all her positive points. Most important, it may help to give your child plenty of time to talk about her feelings and time to tell you why curls are important. Listening is vital!

2. *Analyze expectations.* Carefully analyze your expectations and your child's. Are they realistic? Can you reasonably expect your child to be at the top of the class in math? Perhaps it's more honest to aim at having the child work at his or her peak, regardless of what that level is. Helping a child to do the best work possible for him or her is a real challenge for a parent. It's hard to assess just what a child's ability is; teachers are always glad to work with interested parents in exploring this. It's an important area for home-school cooperation.

3. *Discuss expectations.* Discuss your expectations with your child. Given an opportunity to analyze a problem step-by-step, many children will set goals and solve the problems themselves. Two reasons for this are:
   - It becomes the child's own idea.
   - The step-by-step breakdown helps a child really

look at a problem that may have seemed overwhelming. The child with a math problem may set day-by-day or week-by-week goals in order to be able to see his own progress. This week he will master the multiplication table just for 5s; next week it will be for 6s. Just for today, she will complete her assigned worksheet.

A good self-concept is *learned*. We spend a lifetime in collecting and putting together its pieces. Helping a child grow in confidence and in the assurance that he or she is really all right is a prime responsibility of parenthood and a parent's greatest challenge. The gift of self is not just something we give to a child at birth; we give it to the child every growing day.

The Thinking Parent's Summary for Action

1. Examine your own self-concept. Develop ways to make it more positive.
2. Love your children unconditionally.
3. Encourage your children with *specific* comments.
4. Avoid damaging labels.
5. Set realistic goals for and with your children.
6. Affirm children's efforts to work and think for themselves. Allow for failure when it comes and help the child use the failure as a constructive learning experience.
7. Learn to guide and facilitate rather than always directing.
8. Keep a stroke count.
9. Watch behavior and listen carefully for indications of feelings about self.
10. Don't squelch or deny a child's feelings. Help him (her) think through the difficult or negative emotions and inappropriate actions.
11. Avoid lectures.
12. Help children look at the total picture of themselves.
13. Help children learn constructive, creative self-evaluation.
14. Analyze what matters to both you and your children in terms of your values.
15. Analyze and discuss your expectations and your children's expectations so that children will realistically be better able to succeed.

3

Moral Development

"What Is Right and What Is Wrong?"

It was nothing special, just an inexpensive charm from a chain bracelet. But the charm was cute and it appealed to Kirsten. She was at Elisabeth's house for her Brownie Scout meeting when she noticed it on the floor. She looked around very quickly. No one seemed to be looking, so she picked up the charm and put it in her pocket. She really wanted that charm!

Ten minutes later, Susan began to wail, "I've lost my Garfield charm! I know I had it when I came! I had it when we had a snack. Everybody, please help me find it!" But the charm was nowhere to be found, not in the kitchen or family room. Finally, the Scout Leader asked the girls, "Did anyone see the charm anywhere? Did anyone pick it up? Susan's very upset!"

Kirsten squirmed and looked at the floor. Then she put her hand in her pocket. "I saw something on the floor. I didn't think it belonged to anyone, really. This isn't what you lost, is it?" She took the charm from her pocket and held it out. "I didn't think you meant *this* charm."

Kirsten is in the second grade. She was raised in a sensitive, upright home. She goes to Brownies, church school, and other organizations that expect high moral standards. She was surely raised in a moral environment. What happened? Is this normal?

Presuming that your family values moral development, if I asked, "What do you include in your family value system?" you might list:
- the way we discipline our children
- the way we use leisure time
- the way we spend money
- our attitude toward work
- the behaviors we consider right and wrong.

Values are personal and vary according to culture and family background. Most healthy families have very clear ideas about what is right and what is wrong. Parents in these families may agree on some basic values, but may disagree on certain others. They are, though, open to discussion and respect some variance. There is less concern about whether "Everyone is doing it!" and a real consciousness that "We don't do that in our family!" How does this sense of right and wrong develop in children? How can parents help?

Empathy:
Putting Yourself in Someone Else's Shoes

In our story at the beginning, one of Kirsten's problems was that she wasn't empathetic to Susan and her feeling of loss. One very important part of a well-developed sense of right and wrong is empathy. After all, part of what is wrong with stealing is that it hurts someone. Can we put ourselves in the shoes of the owner? Part of what is wrong with vandalism is that it violates the property of another. Can we put ourselves in the shoes of the owner? Social living demands an understanding of the feelings of others; it demands respect for their rights, their property, their persons; it demands that compromises be made and laws drafted to provide some form of just consideration for everyone. Not everyone can always have his (her) own way. A sense of empathy, then, can help us understand the best ways to live together happily and cooperatively.

Here is how empathy develops:

1. It's all about me! me! me!

The youngest child is sure that because he wants something, the whole world wants him to have it. "I want Billy's truck. I'm going to take it." When Billy starts to cry, the child is genuinely surprised. Didn't Billy want him to have the truck? The fact that Billy has feelings of his own about keeping the truck doesn't occur to the young child. Empathy for Billy still has to be learned. The child may actually experiment with taking things in order to study the reactions of other children. Putting oneself in another's shoes is a more mature skill that is at least partly *learned* as a child becomes developmentally *ready* to learn it.

The development of empathy generally follows a pattern, beginning with the very youngest child's feeling that she (he) is the center of the universe. The young child cannot see things from anyone else's point of view. They are egocentric. They can see issues and events as well as the physical world only from their own perspective.

Kirsten's behavior at least partially fits this stage. "I want the charm. It must be okay for me to have it."

2. What's wrong?

- "I don't know why Susie is crying, but I know she doesn't feel as good as I do."
- "I don't know why Allen doesn't want me to have the ball, but I think he's going to yell if I take it."

The second step toward empathy is an understanding that others may have a different opinion. The child may not know or understand the opinion, but an awareness that there are differences has developed (probably from seemingly endless days of grabbing things away from other children and driving parents over the edge). Kirsten gave an excuse. "I didn't think you meant *this* charm." Others had a different feeling about the charm. She knew Susan was unhappy, so she felt an excuse was necessary.

3. *I sympathize with you!*
   - "I know how sad you feel about your broken doll. I broke mine, too."
   - "Last week I skinned my knee, too. It really hurt!"

The third step is the development of sympathy. People who can sympathize understand how another feels if it is something that they, too, have experienced. The sympathetic stage is a comfortable and valid stage on the way to empathy. Many adults reach this stage and stop.

Even very young children can feel sympathy for others. When one child starts to cry, others in the room will cry. Toddlers will pat a friend on the back or offer them a toy to console them. Parents are wise to build on this strong beginning of concern for others. However, it would be rare for such a child to skip the early stages of egocentrism and *always* be sympathetic.

Kirsten's sympathy had to be triggered by the leader's comments about Susan's unhappiness.

4. *I empathize!*
   - "It must be truly awful to never have enough to eat!" (followed by an effort to help the hungry).
   - "Steve Running Bear isn't being a nerd because he won't look the teacher in the eye. It's a different way of showing respect for the teacher" (followed by an appreciation of other Native American cultural traditions).

Empathy is a word we use far too loosely. It really goes

deeper than sympathy. It means understanding, even when you have never experienced the problem. It means understanding events if they are in a context that is culturally foreign to you. It means truly putting yourself in another's shoes.

> **The Thinking Parent's Summary for Action**
> If you wish to help your children develop empathy—and ultimately a sense of right and wrong—you will:
> 1. Help them to discuss and define their own feelings.
> 2. Help them to compare these feelings to those of others. "How do you think that makes John feel?"
> 3. Help them to care deeply for some*one*, to understand friendships. Don't say, "Of course you like him!" if the child really doesn't. Instead, explore by asking questions. "Why do you like him?" "What is it about her that upsets you so much?" Help your child to analyze and make friendship choices.
> 4. Help them to care deeply for some*thing*. Choose projects that help others, which will encourage empathy, commitment, responsibility. Do not choose *for* the child but *with* the child.
> 5. Model empathetic behavior. Deal empathetically with your children, with your spouse and friends. Choose projects of your own to help others, or work with your children in those the children have chosen.

Moral Development

Empathetic people usually do not hurt others or damage their property. Therefore, the development of empathy is a big step toward understanding right and wrong. Sometimes, however, it is difficult to use empathy alone as a guide for deciding whether something is right or wrong. It is especially difficult when dealing with situations involving a number

of people or with questions related to institutions or businesses. When the individual becomes lost in big business, we find it hard to apply our best principles.
- "The store won't miss it."
- "Who do these things belong to, anyway?"
- "How could the government ever know?"
- "So who could possibly be hurt by my lying about my child's age? I'll save $2."

When children and adults cannot understand how these kinds of cheating ultimately hurt real people, we need rules that simply state that these behaviors are wrong.

Kohlberg's Stages of Moral Development

While part of moral development relates to the development of empathy, it is also a matter of normal growth patterns, including the ability to think logically about abstract ideas. Sometimes it's helpful to have a framework, a way of thinking about an issue. Using the work of Lawrence Kohlberg provides a structure. Kohlberg based his theories on the work of Swiss psychologist Jean Piaget. Kohlberg, whose research covered a twenty-year period, believed that moral development is a progression, a growth through stages. Today we can see problems and inconsistencies in his theories. Does moral development always occur in stages and are they always sequential? We wonder if his ideas of moral stages apply to children from dysfunctional families. However, much that he learned helps us to examine the way children develop a sense of right and wrong.

Stage I

Right and wrong are decided by which authority figure says it and whether or not you get in trouble by doing it.
- "Daddy says that's good, so it must be good."
- "If I get caught, I can't watch TV. I guess it must be a bad thing to do."

Stage II
Right and wrong are based on selfish need. Kirsten was in this stage when she decided that no one would care if she took the charm.
- "It's my toy, so I can do what I want with it."
- "I'll do it if you give me a treat."

Stage III
Right and wrong are based on social approval or on living up to a "good kid" stereotype.
- "How can I face my friends when they find out?"
- "I'll do it if you do it."

Stage IV
Right and wrong are based on socially defined roles and living up to a code designed for the good of all.
- "It was my duty to arrest him."
- "Good parents all do this."
- "I want to be a good citizen."

Stage V
Right and wrong are decided by a moral order which is even above "laws."
- "I don't care if no one else knows. I'll do it because it's right."
- "Everyone deserves a chance."

Young children and primary-age children are Stage I or Stage II. Elementary children would not be expected to get beyond Stage III. Many adults never get beyond Stage IV. Some never get beyond Stage III. Often people behave as if they are in several stages at once as they grow more morally mature.

A Closer Look
Stage I

What happens when a child is in Stage I? This is the stage in which right and wrong are decided according to which authority figure sets the rule and whether or not your action gets you into trouble. Consider these two dilemmas that we might present to children:

- *Story 1.* Suppose that Mark is helping his mother sweep the kitchen. He is awkward with the broom and knocks a tray off the table, including a pitcher of milk and three of his mother's best china cups. Everything breaks. Did Mark do something wrong? (adapted from the studies of psychologist Jean Piaget)

- *Story 2.* Julie is angry. Her father won't let her go out to play. She begins throwing her ball around inside the house. If she can't go out, she'll just throw it around all she wants. She throws harder and harder. Suddenly there is a crash as the ball breaks a cup on the kitchen table. Did Julie do something wrong?

Which child is more guilty? Story 1 is an example of an accident. If Mark was being reasonably careful, we can at least examine his motives and see that he was really trying to help. Story 2 is an example of an accident that occurred because a child was breaking the rules and failing to control emotions.

Adults will look at the motives of the two children. Mark wanted to help; Julie was being naughty. Children will see it differently. If they are in Stage I, they will look at the number of cups broken. The more cups broken, the worse the crime. They will also ask, "Did Mark's parents spank him?" "Did Julie's parents spank her?" If there was punishment, the child was wrong. If not, the child must not have been wrong. Further, the young child will explore the rule: "Did her father say, 'No balls in the house'?" The act is judged on the basis of the broken rule.

In Stage I, children regard rules as if they are huge shade trees that have always been there to cast shadows over their lives. Adults are all-powerful and children must do as they say. The number of cups broken and the amount of punishment are the ways to decide how bad you have been.

Parents who want to help children in this stage may wish to explain motives to the child. However, since the ability to understand motives won't be fully developed until Stage III, parents need to realize that the child may not really absorb all of the meaning. It isn't a bad idea, however, to begin practicing this kind of explanation so that the child can begin to understand as he (she) becomes ready to grasp it.

Though we often tell tiny children to "Be good!" the chances are that the admonition means nothing when they are younger than three. Between age three and approximately ages seven to ten (Stages I and II) "Be good!" means "Avoid all the things you've ever been punished for. Anything you haven't been punished for must be okay (no matter what it is!). If you haven't been punished for it and you really want to do it, go ahead." What an open field for misbehavior!

In our opening story, Kirsten was behaving in transition between stages. She didn't respond until an authority figure directly asked the group if they had seen something on the floor (Stage I). She apparently responded to the feelings of the other child (Stage II).

Part of the parent's explanation must be based on the child's current stage and part should be aimed at helping the child grow into new stages.

- "Julie was wrong. She broke the rule about throwing balls in the house. She will be punished. She knew she was being naughty."
- "Mark was clumsy, but he really was trying to help. We won't punish Mark but we will try to help him sweep without bumping things."

Often, in such a situation, a parent may react with anger

to the apparent size of the crime (the number of cups broken), rather than to the child's intentions. If the parent doesn't sort out motives and punishes on the basis of the number of cups broken, the parent is then acting on the lowest moral stage along with the child.

Also important is the realization that the parent needs to make the punishment fit the crime. If everything is punished as a catastrophe, if everything is equally awful, if all punishments are of equal intensity, children might develop an overblown intensity about being very bad people. They may develop a sense of shame for which they are unable to forgive themselves. In the child's mind, the thing that determines "wrongness" is the punishment. A child might even forget what he (she) did that was wrong and remember only the punishment.

The Thinking Parent's Summary for Action
Stage I

1. Explain everyday situations to your child. Fit the explanation into the child's current stage and also the next stage.
   - Tell the child who was wrong.
   - Tell what rule was broken.
   - Explain the punishment if there is one.
   - Move to Stage II and say, "This is fair because____."
2. Include a discussion of the motive behind the rule and what you perceive as the motive for the child's actions.
3. Stage I children are young. Keep it short!
4. Make the punishment fit the crime in both type and intensity.

Stage II

What happens when a child is in Stage II? In this stage the child's own selfish or egocentric need determines right or wrong. Consider these two situations that we might present to children:

• *Story 1.* Barbara doesn't know her multiplication tables at all. When the teacher gives a test, she copies her neighbor's paper and gets an A. The teacher suspects cheating and confronts Barbara who vehemently denies it.

• *Story 2.* Philip knows most of his multiplication tables but the test has some problems he really doesn't understand. He copies the answers from his neighbor's paper. The teacher assumes he has finally learned the material and doesn't catch the cheating.

Which child was the naughtier? In Stage II the child assumes, selfishly, that his need makes the deed all right. The naughtiness is based on the amount of deviation from truth. Therefore, Barbara was naughtier because she really didn't know any of the material and the teacher caught her. Philip didn't get caught and he really knew most of it anyway. There is apt to be little consideration of cheating as wrong in principle. Kirsten took the charm and reacted as a Stage II child.

In Stage II, children interact on the basis of "That's fair!" but only when they consider it fair for themselves. Fairness may be based on "You scratch my back, I'll scratch yours" rather than on loyalty, gratitude, or justice. They barter and bargain for friendship and favors. They make up game rules that suit themselves and follow standard rules when it is in their own interest to do so.

In Stage I, you can tell a child to go to bed because the "clock says it is time for bed." The child obeys what appears to be an authority. In Stage II, the child wonders, "Why should I go to bed if I don't want to?"

Long-term needs, routines, and principles are either not

understood or are tested. As mentioned, the admonition "Be good!" probably doesn't give the child enough information. "Why is it in my best interests to be good?" "How much can I stray from the rules and still be good?" "What specifically is expected, and is it fair?" Kirsten, for example, responded to the leader when the group was directly asked if they had found the charm. She didn't get caught but apparently decided she ought to confess because Susan was unhappy. She was uncomfortable enough about her action to make up an excuse. Her motivation for taking it, however, was simply that she wanted it.

Usually it works to include several points when reasoning with such a child. Choose some from the previous stage, some from the current stage, and some from the next stage.

- Stage I: "Eight o'clock is bedtime in our house."
- Stage II: "You will feel better and do your math better if you go to bed now."
- Stage III: "It will help us all if you can do this without a fuss."

Children in Stages I and II look upon lies the same way. Outlandish lies in which you are caught are bad. Plausible, possible lies in which you are not caught are not bad. In such cases, you somehow needed to lie.

The Thinking Parent's Summary for Action
Stage II

1. Review the Stage I summary.
2. Plan your explanation to fit into Stage I, the child's current stage, and also a bit from Stage III.
   - From Stage I, tell the child what the rule is and explain the punishment if the rule has been broken.

> - Move to Stage II and say, "This is fair because _____."
> - Give an explanation for the rule, which is based on how it serves the child's own needs.
> - From Stage III, explain what others will think of the child when he (she) complies with the rule.
> 3. Consider motives. Do they affect the evaluation of rightness or wrongness?
> 4. Do not expect more understanding than the child's level of development will allow.
> 5. Make the punishment fit the crime in both type and intensity.

Stage III

In this stage what matters is what others think of you. It is the ultimate peer-pressure stage, a stage in which children want the parent or the teacher to think well of them. But it is also a stage in which behavior is judged by intention, when the child more consistently says, "But he means well!" Also, at this stage the child can judge a friendship on the basis of mutual affection rather than simple usefulness.

The power of adults has shifted from Stage I's disciplinarian to a desire for the adult to like and respect the child. This is the stage at which the child can just begin to truly understand something you have been saying all along: "This is what our family stands for!" It is at Stage III that "Be good!" takes on meanings that say:

- "Do the things that will please your teacher!"
- "Work hard because people will like what they see!"
- "Courtesy and good manners will please Grandpa!"

Stage III encompasses a kind of social awareness that is often, *but not always,* a guide to more responsible behavior. The challenge is to lead the child through this stage of awareness of others so that he (she) pleases others, senses the needs of the class and the family, but then goes a step further. In this next step the child behaves in a positive way *to both please himself or herself and to make the environment more pleasant.*

At Stage III a child begins to see that lying and stealing are naughty, even if they aren't caught and punished. Part of the reason for this is the growing understanding of the meaning of, and necessity for, mutual trust.

If Susan steals her best friend's bracelet and no one catches it, is she naughty? If Amy steals her best friend's bracelet and her friend catches her, is she naughty? Children in Stage III will know that stealing is wrong and that both are naughty. However, they may consider Amy naughtier than Susan because Amy's friend will never like her again. If Susan steals the bracelet so she can trade it for a gift for her mother, Susan's motive would probably be seen as making the theft all right. Stage III people are great rationalizers. What others think of you is the most important thing.

Stage III Story

Eddie has been able to get near the front of the lunch line. When his friend Tom arrives, the line is very long.

Tom promises to give Eddie his ice cream if Eddie will let him into the line.

Children in Stage III will have a hard time sorting out the right and wrong on this issue.

Stage I Responses:
- "Eddie might get in trouble."
- "Eddie should do it because he'll get a free ice cream." (This assumes Eddie isn't caught and, therefore, not punished. The child successfully gets something.)
- "If he doesn't do it, Tom will be mad and will not be his friend." (This is a form of punishment.)

- "If I'm behind Eddie, I won't ever like him again." (This is egocentrism.)

Stage II Responses:
- "It's fair for Eddie because Tom will give him the ice cream." (Personal needs and a fair exchange of favors are the keys. This is different from the Stage I reasoning about the ice cream.)
- "It's not fair to the other kids because they might run out of food for the last person in line." (The personal need of the last child is key here.)
- "People cut in front of us so it's okay for us to take cuts in front of them." (I'll scratch your back if you'll scratch mine.)

Stage III Responses:
- "If Tom and Eddie are best friends, it should be all right for Tom to cut in because friends do things for each other." (Social approval needs are important.)
- "The teacher won't like it." (Please the adult.)
- "If Eddie and Tom were farther back in the line, they wouldn't like having someone cut in." (The "rightness" of a behavior is judged by what is or is not condoned by others.)
- "It isn't fair to cut in front of people in lines."

In order to deal with a Stage III child, it is important to know just a bit about the next stages so they can be encouraged and recognized when they occur. However, Stages IV and V are models of later adolescence and adulthood. They will be mentioned here only so you can get a total picture. They aren't likely to show up in an elementary-age child.

Stage IV
This is a "law and order" stage. We obey rules to maintain the social order. We do our duty because the "law is good." Moral behavior comes from the law.

Stage V
This is the stage when commitment to conscience and the rights and dignity of all persons are uppermost. Laws come from moral behavior. Democratic behavior can change laws.

Stage IV Responses:
- "Eddie would be breaking a rule to let his friend in line."
- "If everyone did that, then they would be breaking the rules."
- "You shouldn't break a rule to help a friend." *

When we discuss moral dilemmas with children, we may find many instances when they seem to be thinking on a higher level because they give what appears to be the "right" answer. It is very important to have children understand the reasons why the behaviors in question are right or wrong. In the story of Eddie and Tom, we have seen that a child might consider it wrong to be cutting in line—but without a real understanding of why. The child could say it is wrong for the "wrong reason." As noted before, to help children grow, explain situations with reasons that fit several stages of moral development. Realize that at least part of the explanation must be at the child's current stage. A very small part of the parent's explanation can be one stage higher to help the child stretch and grow. Remember also that the parent's behavior should be at a higher level than the child's. How else will the child have models to evaluate?

---

* Adapted from Peter Scharf, William McCoy, Diane Ross, *Growing Up Moral* (Minneapolis, Minn.: Winston Press, 1979), pp. 54-59.

> **The Thinking Parent's Summary for Action Stage III**
>
> 1. Review the summaries for Stages I and II.
> 2. Plan your explanation to fit into the child's current stage, but also Stages I and II. Include a little of the next stage, too.
>   - "This is the rule."
>   - "This is fair because_____."
>   - "This will make others feel_____."
>   - "These are the needs of your friends and family___."
>   - Stage IV: "If everyone did this, the school or home would not run well." Rules are important.
> 3. Include consideration of motives and why they are or are not the main consideration.
> 4. You are a model for your child's moral behavior. On which level are you functioning?

Often we expect a higher level of moral thinking and behavior than our child's developmental stage will allow. This is confusing to children. They may not understand our expectations or our displeasure at their behavior. And often we complicate things by modeling behavior that is on a lower level than the child's.

While the stage theory described here is only one of many approaches to moral development, it does help us to get a handle on some of the ways children think and behave. It is a way to begin.

Suggestions for the Thinking Parent

Moral behavior is learned from what children see and hear around them.

1. Parents need to think through the ways they will explain right and wrong to their children. Knowing a little of the way the child thinks at a particular age helps you to get the message through.
2. Examine the rules you follow, the excuses you make for yourself, the kind of right and wrong behavior you model for your child.
3. Help your child to make choices and to learn the consequences of those choices.
4. Examine motives when you judge behavior, and help your child to do so.
5. Talk about the importance of rules.
6. Talk and behave with an understanding of the rights and needs of all humanity and of the importance of a world order that respects these.
7. And, finally, in your moral education journey, give your child some guidelines. Help your child to feel that your family stands for certain things. This does not mean dictating to children what they are to believe without helping them learn to make choices and think through the issues. However, we all need models, starting points, mentors, and guides—and we all need standards for analyzing our experiments in human relations.

4

DEVELOPING INTERNAL CONTROL

"Who's in Charge Here?"

Consider these two children, Kristi and Kyle:
- Kristi is having trouble with her friend next door. She doesn't know what to do about it. Her reaction is to sit in the corner of her room sulking and hugging one of her old teddy bears. The behavior continues for a week. Her parents can't get her to discuss it.
- Kyle wants to join a group on the playground. When they ignore him on Tuesday, he comes with his new football to share on Wednesday. When that doesn't work, he tries a different tactic on Thursday. He quietly stands near the group, listening to the conversation so he can join in when it's appropriate. By Friday he's figured out a way to be a group member.

Kristi doesn't think she has any control over the situation. Kyle is willing to make an effort. What is the difference in the attitudes of these two children? Basically, it's a question of whether a child assumes that he (she) has any decision-making skills and any ability or right to carry them out. In other words, how much power and what kind of power does the child have? This is a simplistic explanation for what researchers call "locus of control."

Internal Control

When a person has an internal locus of control, they believe that they can influence what happens to them. This is true of both children and adults. If you work in a place where your opinions are respected and where you are expected to help with the decision making, you feel you have some degree of control. When things go wrong, in many cases you will come up with ideas for fixing them. You feel responsible for the results. You work harder. You know that sitting around and waiting for someone else to fix it will waste *your* time and the time of all the other workers.

Children with an internal locus of control know that the way they do their assignments influences the way they feel about the class. For these children "success breeds success." This means that these are children who understand that *they alone* are responsible for doing well on the math test or finishing a good science project. When the teacher says they have done well, they are proud of their efforts and willing to try again on the next assignment. They know that they can make things happen.

External Control

People who have an external locus of control do not feel they have any power to change their world. They don't know what choices they have. In the adult work world, these people are the ones who never do anything on their own. They don't feel they have any rights or any abilities. Someone or something has power over them.

Children who have an external locus of control assume

that luck or fate is responsible for their situation. If others don't like them, they assume it's someone else's fault. They are unable to understand their own role in making and keeping friends. They don't know how to make decisions about their own behavior and then act on them.

Developing Internal Control

Researchers have outlined some of the characteristics of people with internal control. They consider these people more productive. These competent people have:
- a strong curiosity about life
- goals for living
- a balance between independence and the ability to live and work well with others
- a positive relationship with family and friends.

What does this mean for children?

Developing Curiosity in Children

Curious children want to know how things work. They want to know about the natural world and its people and explore the knowledge and arts of the world. Curious children are very aware of things around them, exploring and asking questions. They are busy in either physical or mental activity.

Curious children can be hard to live with, however. They get into things and make messes and have endless projects and collections. They ask many questions and require a good deal of wisdom and patience from their parents.

Obviously, they cannot be allowed to experiment with everything or take everything apart, or to flit uncontrollably from idea to idea. The trick is to determine what limits and rules are reasonable for curious children. What can they be encouraged to do on their own? They can't, though, be allowed to feel that they are a success because they have successfully wrecked the living room.

Children with an internal locus of control feel capable because they have been given many chances to experiment with their world; they have positive goals.

Setting Goals

Children have to have goals for their lives, just as adults do. What good is it to be curious if it is not connected somehow to worthwhile goals? Hurting others or tearing up the house are not worthwhile goals. What good is a child's acceptance into a gang if the gang is always in trouble, experiments with drugs, or does very little except hang out at the mall? Human beings need to feel that they have abilities, that they are worthwhile, and that they can accomplish what they set out to do. Children with no goals or with poor goals may not have any idea about what they can do. No one has helped them to analyze their desires and abilities or helped them to choose realistic heroes or models for living.

Children have to understand that the adults in their lives have positive goals, and be able to decide on their own needs, desires, and goals. They need to be able to examine the goals of their gangs, as well. And then they need to figure out how these fit together.

Developing Positive Relationships

Children who have an internal locus of control are not easily manipulated. They feel that their ideas and opinions matter; they learn to express them and negotiate so that others will agree or at least respect them. They fit in socially and are often leaders in their group. In addition, they can feel secure working alone if they need to or wish to.

The problem with this *could* be that the child might seek out a group where he (she) can be in control, even if it isn't a group with desirable ideas and goals. This means that the child's need for control has warped his (her) goals. On the other hand, very gifted children may try to push ideas that are too mature or offbeat for the gang. Acceptance in the gang means that the child must become a follower rather than a leader.

Children need to learn to balance their goals, their social skills, and their behavior at home and with their friends.

What Can Parents Do?
　1. *Examine your parenting style.*
　　• Do your parenting skills match your child's personality, age, and needs?
　　• Are you a warm and loving parent? Do you touch and speak with love? Everyone gets mad sometimes, but do the good times outweigh the bad? Internal control grows in a warm, loving family.
　　• Is your discipline consistent? Do your rules make sense?
　2. *Encourage curiosity.*
　　• Set reasonable limits on messes and explorations.
　　• Provide work spaces for projects even if you live in a small apartment.
　　• Be willing to help seek out resources and materials, use the library, look up answers.
　　• Either turn off the TV or use it to find interesting new programs and ideas.
　3. *Be role models.*
　　• Model positive goals. Examine your own goals in life. When you are ready, let your children know about them.
　　• Be aware that children will sense your goals and values, even if you say little about them. We act on our beliefs, even if we don't mean to. Children learn from what they see us do!
　　• Be concerned about what your child is learning and doing in school. Your involvement is a model of concern for education.

- How do you meet the world? Are you upbeat and positive or always crabby and worried? Your attitude may become your child's.
- What kind of problem solver are you? Children who see their parents solving problems will try to be that way too.

4. *Develop support networks.*
    - Who do you turn to when you need help, friendship, and guidance? Everyone needs to feel they have a place where they belong and someone cares. Start with your spouse if you are married, or with extended family if you are parenting alone. Then reach out to friends, religious, or community groups.
    - Help your child develop a support network. Start with yourselves as parents and then help your child look for caring young friends and adults. Be available!

We cannot control our whole world. There are people so enmeshed in the cycle of poverty and governmental failure that they no longer have control. There are people who are stuck in bad jobs, bad marriages, bad financial situations. They are paralyzed by both the system and their own despair. But those people most apt to struggle out of their difficulties and solve their problems are people who were raised from childhood to believe that they are capable and that there might be a solution somewhere.

Those who make it have an internal locus of control. They believe that they have within themselves the ability to make a difference in their own worlds.

The Thinking Parent's Summary for Action

To develop a sense of internal control and the ability to influence what happens in his (her) world:

1. Encourage your child's curiosity.
   - Encourage your child's own interests.
   - Provide work space and set limits on messes and experiments.
   - Be aware of your world and teach this to your child.
   - Look for materials.
2. Help your child to set desirable goals.
   - Emphasize the child's strengths. Work with him (her) to improve areas of weakness.
   - Analyze the relationship between the child's goals and the child's abilities.
3. Help your child develop positive relationships by helping her (him) balance group control or power with abilities and goals.
4. Examine your parenting style.
   - Are you warm, consistent?
   - Is your style appropriate for the child's developmental stage?
5. Be a role model.
   - Examine your own goals.
   - Analyze the way you meet the world. Are you upbeat or defeated?
   - Be involved in your child's education.
   - Model good problem-solving skills.
6. Develop a support network of friends and advisors so your child will learn how to find support and ideas.
7. Be available to your child!

5

COMMON COURTESY

Simple—But Uncommon—
Words Today

We often look at the children who tear through our homes daily and comment in total exasperation, "If only they had a little common courtesy!"

We offer cookies and watch the neighbor's children (and our own) grab them without a word of thanks. We watch the neighbor's children (and our own) crowd past us to sit closer to the TV—blocking our view—all without a word of excuse. We watch our sister's children (and our own) tear open the gifts of Hanukkah and Christmas, stopping only long enough to say "Yuk!" at Aunt Susan's gift of a sweater.

A little common courtesy? But, as we all know, courtesy is far from common! These days it's a rare and *un*common commodity.

Many of today's parents are the product of the free-wheeling 1960s when the rules of conduct were viewed quite differently. Those were the days when some parents were concerned that too many rules could stifle creativity. Some felt that the way to avoid having rebellious children was to have fewer rules and make fewer demands. These children of that decade are raising their own children now, but they have difficulty deciding which habits, manners, and rules of conduct are appropriate. After all, times have changed and the expectations are different from the time when they were growing up.

But that isn't the whole story! Many of us *were* raised to have good manners but find it difficult to convince our children that courtesy is important. Well-mannered children may be labeled as nerds by their peers. They see the opposite behavior on television. They meet ill-mannered store clerks who were never taught that the store is selling *service*. Computers seldom say "Please!" and "Thank You!" Parents and teachers who should be models of behavior are in a hurry to get to the next scheduled event and don't bother excusing themselves for intruding on the time of another. The world moves too fast to take time for manners.

What are some reasonable courtesies for children to learn? Here are three basic courtesies with which to begin:

Learning to Say "Please"

An amazing number of children believe that acquiring things is their inalienable right. We live in a product-oriented culture in which children are assaulted daily with commercials for all the things they must have to be popular, beautiful, and happy. The product battle is waged before children are old enough to have their own money. They think, therefore, that it is all right to spend ours. Years ago the commercial aspects of the world were less evident until a child was old enough to earn money. The earliest "wants" might have been something like a bicycle or the fabulous doll in the store window.

How different it is today! Every movie has an entire store

full of special toys to go with it. Some television shows are actually 30-minute commercials. In many cases a child doesn't even see money being given in exchange for these wonderful products. What they see is the magic of a plastic card that seems to be usable without any limit.

Is it any wonder that children do not understand how to express a desire for something? They feel that these products are out there for anyone to grab; they can have them without hardly even asking. Mom and Dad use this world of products to provide surprises when they come home from extended business trips. Besides, if parents feel guilty about being away, a gift seems like a logical way to say "I'm sorry!" And don't forget the use of all kinds of products as bribes for good behavior. The world moves too fast to *reason* with children. We bribe them to do *what* we want *when* we want it!

Learning to be courteous when expressing a desire for something should begin very young. Whining and demanding are inappropriate. Fulfilling some of our child's desires may mean that a parent spends time and energy as well as money. Early in life, children should understand how special such favors can be.

Children, therefore, should:

1. *Express desires and even needs using the word "Please."*

2. *Learn how to present a case for real needs or wants.* This is the valuable art of negotiation. Even young children can come up with three good reasons why they need something. Parents must define what they mean by "good reasons."

3. *Learn when to stop asking.* The burden for this lies with the parent (see below). The child should learn that "Please" doesn't guarantee that the child gets what he (she) wants.

4. *Learn that the word "Please" is not just for things* but also for requested actions, help, privileges, etc.

Parents should, therefore:

1. *Ignore requests that aren't preceded with "Please" and expressed courteously.*

2. *Define what is meant by a "good reason."*
   - Is it a good reason if everyone in the neighborhood has one?
   - Is it a good reason if the child says he (she) will take good care of it?
   - Can you count on the child to be interested in it for a long time, even if he (she) says it will last forever?
   - Is it a good reason if the child says she (he) will pay for it?

3. *Teach the child when to stop asking.* After the child has presented a case, it is up to the parent. Either give a response or indicate that you will think about it. Specify how long you will think about it. The child's age will determine how long you can put off a response. Give the child some idea of when to expect an answer. After that, you need to express some finality. "I've thought about it and the answer is no!"

4. *Explain their thinking.* Give reasons for your decision. What fits your home and budget? What fits the child's age and long-term interests?

5. *Not allow themselves to be nagged into giving in.* If you change your mind, it should be for a good reason. Maybe the child has renegotiated and done so convincingly. Maybe your situation has changed.

6. *Realize that their time is also a gift to their child.* Help your child to understand this. Remember, however, that your time is not a gift if you have given it grudgingly. If you respect your *child's* time and thank her (him) for giving it, your child will be more apt to understand *your* gift of time. It's all right to explain to your child that you have given him (her) a gift of time.

7. *Always be a model for their child.* Use "Please" when making requests of the child or another family member. Your child will be more apt to do what he (she) sees you doing.

Learning to Say "Thank You"

Children should be expected to say "Thank you" when they are given anything. This includes everything from passing them the butter to giving them their allowance. It means expressing gratitude for even small gifts. Since getting things is not the child's inalienable right, the child needs to learn to appreciate the things that are given.

Learning to say "Thank you" is really a first step in learning gratitude. It's a social nicety. It may even require a form of play-acting. A child learns to say "Thank you" as a habit, regardless of whether he (she) feels much gratitude. It's important for a child to learn to tell Uncle Joe that he really appreciates the baseball glove, even though the child hates baseball, knows he's a klutz, and really wants to spend his life as a journalist. Uncle Joe did, after all, give the child a gift and gifts are not a requirement for unclehood.

Learning gratitude is the subject for another essay. It takes more training and more empathetic thinking about people and values to understand gratitude. Being able to understand Uncle Joe's inappropriate gift may mean understanding Uncle Joe's background, time of life, and experience with children. Children need to learn how to feel gratitude, but, as a courtesy, they first need to learn to at least say "Thank you."

Children, therefore, should:

1. *Say "Thank you" with notes or phone calls for each and every gift.* Mom or Dad should not write the note for the child. The notes the child writes should be presentable. The length should be determined by the age of the child. Laziness is no excuse for a one-line note from an older child.

2. *Understand that they should say "Thank you," even if the gift isn't something they particularly like.*

3. *Be able to pretend real appreciation in situations where more than a "Thank you" is required.*

4. *Appreciate thoughtful actions, friendly attitudes, and loving*

family and friendships. Children need to begin to notice the positive behaviors of others. These will be their models.

Parents should, therefore:

1. *Expect that thank you notes will be written before the gift item can be used.* For young children the note may be a picture that the child has drawn with words dictated to the parent. Older children need not have every word written as an adult would write, but they can be expected to do the job themselves. It is helpful, as children begin to develop the thank you habit, for parents to discuss with the child what he (she) wants to say. Suggestions from the parent should not be dictates, but should be taken seriously by the child.

2. *Teach the child how to express appreciation without lying.* Children need to understand the difference between *liking the gift* and *liking the person and the thoughtfulness.* They can honestly tell a thoughtful neighbor that "It was nice of you to bake me some cookies on my birthday!" even though they hate date bars.

3. *Teach the child to look at the giver as well as the gift.* Grandpa has no way of knowing what a child of today might want. Aunt Bea is on a limited income and any gift at all is a gift of the heart.

4. *Always be a model for their child.* Say "Thank you" when anyone gives you something or does something for you. Write thank you notes and let your child see you doing so. Express appreciation for thoughtfulness in the same way your children are being taught to understand thoughtfulness. Your child will be more apt to do what he (she) sees you doing.

Learning to Say "Excuse Me"

"Excuse me!" means that a person realizes that something he (she) is doing or has done is disruptive. It's an apology for rudeness or thoughtlessness. It may be used as a way of saying, "I really am sorry to bother you but...!" This cour-

tesy means that a child is able to put herself (himself) in someone else's shoes. It means that the child is able to think:
- "I'm standing in John's way. Now he can't see the TV screen."
- "I'm talking too loudly. Now mom can't hear on the phone."
- "I'm being too crabby. It's making everyone else miserable."
- "If I make my way to that seat in the middle, I have to disturb four people. But it's the only way to get to there."

A mechanical list of situations requiring an "Excuse me" might be a first step. With young children, a parent makes a very short list. As children get older, more situations are added. While the child is learning to put himself (herself) into someone else's shoes, the response is becoming a habit.

Being able to understand how our actions are affecting someone else is a vital next step and the beginning of thoughtfulness. Some children seem to naturally notice and have concern for others, but many must actually be taught this awareness. This doesn't mean that there is something wrong with the child; it's part of development. We all know that there are developmental differences between children, even in the same family. If a child does not intuitively put herself (himself) in another's shoes, the parent can help the child to learn.

Children, therefore, should:

1. Learn the mechanical rules for saying "Excuse me" when they are in someone's way or causing a disruption. This may or may not accompany any real understanding about other people's feelings but simply be an habitual response.

2. Learn to wonder how others are feeling. They need to ask themselves, "Am I doing something to make this person uncomfortable?" or "What is my friend thinking?" They can practice reading facial expressions and body language.

3. Learn ways to respond if they are, in fact, causing discomfort. Is saying "Excuse me" enough? Maybe there is something the child needs to do to make things right again. Does the spilled juice need to be wiped up? Does the child need to find a different seat in front of the television or help rearrange the chairs? Some action may be required.

Parents should, therefore:

1. Think of situations that might arise when an "Excuse me" is appropriate. Discuss these with the child and perhaps write them down. Have a short list for younger children and add to it according to the child's developmental stage.

2. Ask their child, "How would you feel if that happened to you?" or "How do you think Kristin is feeling?" Begin early to help them put themselves in another's shoes.

3. Teach their child the consequences of their actions toward others. "If you _____, then_____ will happen." Then go on to explain if the child needs to say "Excuse me" or apologize in some way.

4. Help their child to think through any actions that might be required. Some of the actions may be common sense, but don't assume that they are common sense for a child.

5. Be a model for their child. Remember to say "Excuse me" to your child and other family members. When other family members are courteous, it will be easier for your child to know when these behaviors are appropriate.

Unless parents are models of courteous behavior, our children will never learn common courtesy. We have examined three simple points of courtesy with which the children should begin:

1. Learning to say "Please."
2. Learning to say "Thank you."
3. Learning to say "Excuse me."

In each case I have suggested the parents as models. Parents need to think through the many demands that are made in a family on any given day. "Make your bed!" "Set the table!" "Brush your teeth!" The more hurried our lives, the more strident the demands. We may feel we have no time for courtesy. It is true that by the second or third request we have to resort to a firmer way of speaking. By that time, parents need to apply additional ways of communicating and disciplining so that they aren't simply nagging. Courtesy, however, is an indispensable element of our behavior. Sometimes it helps to be able to say, "I have been courteous with you. What should be your courteous response?"

Of course, it won't always work! But if you begin on the highest note, a few lapses will hardly carry you and your children into rude thoughtlessness. With no goals or ideals about courtesy, you and your children may get mired in some unpleasant, anti-social habits. *Common courtesy begins with uncommonly courteous parents.*

The Thinking Parent's Summary for Action

These are three things the thinking parent will wish to remember to teach a child: the common courtesies.

Saying "Please"

- Teach children to say "Please" along with the proper and polite way to ask for things.
- We don't owe children everything they want. Help children to sort out the difference between needs and wants.
- Teach children when to stop asking.
- Don't give in to the child's nagging.
- Say "Please" when making requests of your child.

Saying "Thank You"
- Children should write or phone their own thank you for each gift.
- Teach children to notice and appreciate the thoughtful actions of others.
- Help children to understand the importance of saying "Thank you," even if they don't like the gift.
- Learn to appreciate the giver as well as the gift.
- Thank your child for the things they do for you. Model gratitude!

Saying "Excuse Me"
- Help children develop the habit of saying "Excuse me."
- Teach children to notice and be concerned about the way their behavior affects others.
- Teach children other appropriate responses when they are causing discomfort.
- Model courteous concern for others, including your children.

6

YOUR CHILD AND WORK

The Hard Work
of Developing Helpful Children

Do these three situations sound familiar?
- Melissa has just finished making her lunch and you wonder if any peanut butter ended up on the bread. Most of it seems to have been left on the counter top. And Melissa? She's left, too!
- It's Saturday—your only free day! You are now free to do the cleaning, shopping, and laundry. Your children are also free. And that's just about what they're worth to you right now!
- You need to have the lawn mowed. Your children are on another planet!

Do your children help at home? (Silly question?) Do you wonder what chores are reasonable for a school-age child? Is it a real tug-of-war to get your child to finish a job? Is it easier to do it yourself? I don't intend to list a lot of specific chores, but only to suggest that work may be just the tonic your child needs to build character.

There are some very good developmental reasons why work is important for your school-age child. The years between seven and ten have been called the years of "industry." Psychoanalyst Erik Erikson tells us that in this stage children experience a drive toward productive use of energy. They have many skills that they want to practice and use; they want to feel competent and grown up. If this drive is not satisfied, they develop feelings of inferiority and incompetence.

So if your child is supposed to be developmentally programmed to be industrious, why does she (he) appear lazy? Did this intellectual giant, Erikson, ever really *see* a kid? Why does your child say "Wait a minute!" when you ask that a job be done? Why does your child say "That's boring!" when you assign a chore? Or "Whyyy meeee?" Or worse, not answer at all! For starters, here are some explanations:

- "Wait a minute!" may mean that the child really is concentrating—on something else. It may not be what you want her to concentrate on, but, developmentally she's on target.
- "That's boring!" Maybe it is boring!
- "Whyyy meeee?" Have you explained the division of responsibilities in your home?
- No answer! It may be a way to appear invisible, or a way to get time to think up an excuse, or a way to wait to see if you'll give up and do the job for him.

Children aren't going to jump at the chance to do chores. Do you? But they do respond reasonably well to those activities that have become a habit, tradition, or expectation in their homes. If you haven't made work a part of your family expectations, then now is the time to do so!

Changes in expectations cannot be made overnight. If

you haven't expected your child to do chores regularly, then developing the new habits and routines will take time. If you haven't made it clear that you expect perseverance, then trusting your child to finish a job will also take time. Here are some ideas to start you thinking.

Work and Your Child's Development

Developmentally, in this stage of "industry," the school-age child wants to practice and master a skill, usually one he *wants* to master. When homework is related to a subject the child enjoys, he will do it more willingly. So too, if the home chore is one he enjoys, he is more apt to do it without being nagged. So the first problem facing the parent is doing a good marketing job. Take a cue from marketers of toothpaste; they find ways to make a dull habit interesting. The child needs to be motivated to do something that is usually not appealing. Motivation may not be in the form of actually enjoying the job itself, but in knowing that it's important, expected, and something he can do well.

Building something or completing a project can be a real joy. But children absorbed in working to complete it will usually pull the "wait-a-minute!" game. They are busy; they have a drive to finish. And, yes, the drive to persevere is hooked to their interest in the project. But it may not be a project on the *parent's* agenda. Parents aren't always reasonable about the way they interrupt children. Granted, they often need to have a child come *right now*, but often a little warning may be possible. This shows respect for the child. If a parent wants the child's respect, then the parent should respect the child. The child considers his time to be valuable, too. Parents don't like to be interrupted, so why should children like it?

Once the skill is mastered and the job completed, the child feels that repetition is boring. That's why it's hard to get children to drill on multiplication tables. And, similarly, they think a home chore is boring once they have mastered it. The problem is that they don't always know when they have mastered the skill or the facts. Frequent check-ups are necessary to tell how they're doing. Otherwise, they may not know *how well* they've done, or *when* they are done. If they haven't done a satisfactory job, the approach to mastery should be varied to overcome boredom.

In this stage, children want to do real work, acting like real adults: real baking, real mending, real painting, real cleaning. They also need structure and order. They love to collect things, line them up, group them, display them. Use their need for structure to help them in ordering and structuring their rooms. Remember that rules are also a form of structure. The child's need for rules is part of your decision about a time when a chore should be done. The way you state your specific expectations is also part of the rule making in your home.

The Family as a Small Business

The family is a small institution, or, perhaps, in some ways like a small business. To make it work, all members must have a role—job descriptions, as it were. All members must feel that their particular job is necessary. Does your child feel like an important, contributing part of the family, playing a needed role? This is the foundation of all other suggestions—the first rule related to family work. How do you make your child feel loved, wanted, and needed?

Make Your Child Feel Needed

Help children to understand that work does not get done by magic. If the house is always cleaned after they go to bed, if their clothes get picked up without their having to lift a finger, if the picnic happens whether or not they help out, children get the feeling that their efforts are not required to get things done.

1. Sometimes it's helpful to let natural consequences take effect. If the clothes aren't picked up, eventually there are no clean clothes to wear. If the toys aren't picked up, they are taken away. This has to be carefully handled. Sometimes natural consequences can drive the parent insane before they take effect. (The pile of dirty clothes starts to mildew and you wish you could move out.)

2. A second approach is to have a family meeting (see point 3) to discuss what it means to be a family. Ask the family members to describe what they think a family is. You might even want to write down the responses. Guide the discussion so that it includes some things that family members do for each other. Ask: How do things get done in a family home? Whose job is it to_____?

Next, list chores that need to be done around the house. Find out which family members know how to do those chores. Help the children see that many of the chores are things they are competent to do. You are now ready to think through the following material and develop a system for actually getting the chores done.

3. Let children share in the decision making. If children share in the decision making and the planning, they will also understand more fully their share in the work that makes the family function. Holding family council meetings and discussing the needs of the family and the ways to solve family problems is a first step. Sometimes it means just fifteen minutes after dinner once a week. Sometimes meetings are more formal or more frequent. But the key is the involvement of each family member in defining problems and in carrying out family plans.

Defining Expectations

1. How much can you expect of your child? Are you expecting too little or too much? Talk to your friends and your child's teacher about this. Get some ideas about the kinds of help you might expect from your child. Your child's age and stage of development should be a guide. Is your child strong enough to push the mower? Is she old enough to understand the safety problems related to a power mower? Is he able to do more than vacuum the middle of the room?

With very young children, you may find it worthwhile to provide special equipment so that the child can do the job. For example, use unbreakable tableware or assign the child to handle only unbreakable items. Shorten the wand on the vacuum cleaner to one section instead of the usual two. Have a few smaller sponges for small hands. Have a small laundry basket the child can carry alone.

2. *Train your child to do the job.* Sometimes we assume that everyone knows how to sweep a floor or dust a table. Does your child really know how to systematically run the vacuum over each section of the rug? Does he (she) know on which shelf you expect the toys to be stored? Have you showed your child how to load the dishwasher so that the water will reach each item? Have you given instructions for sorting clothes for the washer? Take time to work with her (him) and give careful guidance and suggestions. In the long run, time spent in training is saved later on.

3. *Don't expect perfection.* Most children haven't had enough experience to do perfect work. This does not mean, however, that you accept poor workmanship. Know the difference between the child doing the very best job he (she) can, and getting away with sloppy or partially completed work.

Children can get very discouraged if they always hear "That's fine, honey, but_____." On the other hand, they will soon feel that you are an easy mark if you accept work they really know is inferior. One trick is to ask, "Do you see anything here that you could have done better?" Another is to first list specifically the parts of the job you consider completed and completed well. "You sorted the socks just right. Thank you! Now you need to finish the underwear." Or try

"I appreciate the work you *have* done. You had better give the table another swipe with the sponge so it will be really clean."

Sharing the Load
Find out which jobs are really boring or distasteful. Maybe the family discussion needs to include an understanding that some necessary jobs will always be boring. Does one child always have the same job? Is it possible to do some trading of jobs? Are some tasks more challenging than others? Can children do some choosing?

Of course, one problem is that trading can result in arguments.
- "It isn't my turn! I did it last week!"
- "I always end up doing your job and mine, too!"

Too much choice and too many weekly changes can mean that the job doesn't really belong to anyone. No one takes responsibility to see that it is done and done well. However, the fact is that some jobs are unpopular. These should be divided according to degree of challenge and degree of distaste or boredom. A very few jobs might be traded weekly and a written schedule posted to eliminate arguments.

The discussion can also include some efforts to alleviate the boredom. Are there ways to make jobs more interesting:
- Is there a favorite tape that might be played while your child is working?
- Is there something to look forward to when the work is done?
- Can the child pretend to be cleaning out Princess Diana's royal residence or the Ninja Turtles' hideout?

The Parent as Executive
As the parent, are you also a good executive? Are you considerate? Grateful? Are you exploitative? A nag? There are

ways to criticize and ways not to. Here are ideas for constructive criticism.

1. *Focus on the work, not the worker.* Instead of saying "You're sloppy," try saying, "There's still dirt on the rug and a pile of books to put on the shelf."

2. *Describe what still needs to be done and how it needs to be done.* Instead of saying, "That's a lousy job," try saying, "You will be finished when you wipe____and pick up ____. Thank you." Telling a child *how* to improve will gain more cooperation than calling him (her) uncomplimentary names. Think of the ways you would prefer to have your supervisor deal with *you*; then treat your child with the same consideration.

3. *Keep your expectations in line with the child's abilities and stage of development.* We've already discussed this; it's part of being a good parent executive. Well-defined expectations can help the child to develop good self-esteem. The child needs to know that sloppy work is not all right. He (she) needs to develop a sense of pride in jobs well done, and to succeed often. *Strike a balance!* There's no pleasing some parents! Nothing is ever good enough! The child must not feel that no matter how hard he (she) works, no matter what effort is put into the job, the parent is never satisfied. Good self-esteem is built when a child feels this way:

- "I am capable of doing this job!"
- "They trust me to do this job!"
- "I have done this job well!"

4. *Be respectful and courteous.* Parents are often demanding. Saying "Please" and "Thank you" are simple ways to do this. Granted, these go out the window when the child ignores you or procrastinates. Then more firmness is needed. But at least begin with courtesy. That's how you'd like your supervisor to treat *you*.

A recent study reported that "the willingness and capacity to work during childhood is the most important forerunner—more than native intelligence, social class, or family situation—of mental health in adulthood." *

Think about the working atmosphere in your home.
- Is it a good training ground for future work habits and skills?
- Is it a pleasant place to work?
- Are you developing mentally healthy adults for the future?

The Thinking Parent's Summary for Action

To develop helpful children:

1. Make the child feel needed.
   - Help your child to understand what happens when certain jobs aren't done.
   - Include your child in planning work schedules.
2. Define expectations.
   - Determine how much you can reasonably expect.
   - Train your child to do the job the right way.
   - Don't expect perfection.
3. Share the load.
   - Determine boring or distasteful jobs.
   - Figure out ways to alleviate boredom or equalize the number of unpopular jobs for each person.
4. Be an effective executive.
   - Criticize constructively. Focus on the work, not on character. Describe what needs to be done.
   - Keep in mind the child's abilities, age, and stage of development.
   - Be respectful and courteous.

---

*Dava Sobel, *New York Times* Service, "Early Work Habits Show Mental Health," published in *Minneapolis Tribune*, Nov. 15, 1981. Report of a study by George and Caroline Vaillant, Harvard, Mass.

7

FAMILY RITUALS AND TRADITIONS

Building Memories
and Cementing Values

What did you look forward to as a child? Were there certain weekly or annual events that held special meaning for you?

I remember looking forward to the annual Boy Scout ice cream social. It was a special event for my Scout Leader father and much-admired older brother. I felt privileged to be allowed into that world for one night. Besides, it was held at the Scout Troop cabin. I remember childhood summers in a funny leaky tent by Lake Erie where we made popcorn over a kerosene stove and entertained the neighborhood children when it rained. With my own four boys, I remember the hilarious Christmas treasure hunts that stretched gift-giving to a full day or more as we ran all over the neighborhood in search of clues. Birthdays meant baking a cake symbolic of the child's interests that year, a sort of cake diary of their growing up. And when we lived in north Florida, the rituals included regular explorations of the springs and rivers by raft or tube or canoe.

December is a good time to think about family rituals and traditions. But these special activities are important all year—not just for December! Rituals, traditions, and regularly scheduled special events are important to all of us. Because we are a family, they provide us with memories that are like a glue holding us together. They provide us with stability and security; they help us know what to expect.

Adults Need Traditions and Rituals

Adults need traditions and rituals because:

1. *Rituals provide stability.* Our world is fast-paced and often impersonal. People come and go in our neighborhood and church. In our work places, which may be large and automated, we deal with so many customers or co-workers that the faces blur together. We may not know whether our job is secure. It's important, then, to have a few things we can count on.

Sometimes the stability is provided by a simple ritual like dinner together each night. We need to know that there will be a moment to read the paper, baked beans on Saturday night, a comfortable old sweat suit to relax in, or the same loving greeting: "Hi, honey! How was your day?"

2. *Rituals may help us to slow down.* Rituals and traditions can serve to slow us down and help us reflect. These might include meditation or prayer, writing diaries and journals, writing to or calling friends, visiting neighbors, browsing at a museum, and many others. These activities become rituals when we do them often, perhaps on a predictable schedule, and we look forward to the breather they provide in our lives. They can provide a restful routine by being repeated so often that we don't need to think much about them.

3. *Rituals and traditions give us something to look forward to.* It may be lunch once a week with special friends, poker or

bridge with the gang, TV football with neighbors. Sometimes it's an annual hunting trip or a visit to a relative. Sometimes it's holiday parties or religious events the whole family looks forward to. Whatever it is, the event would be missed if it were eliminated. It's a part of who we are.

4. *Traditions add color and magic to a very "daily" world.* They enrich our lives and make them more meaningful. We store them away in our memory banks so we can recall them later to refresh us; they are important parts of our lives.

Children Need Traditions and Rituals

Children need rituals and traditions for all of the same reasons that adults need them.

1. *Children need rituals to give stability to their speeded-up lives.* Because children grow fast, the changes in their minds and bodies may be confusing them. They may feel that rules are arbitrary and that expectations are too high. It's comforting, then, to be able to know that at the end of the day there will be, for example, a family story time and quiet talk.

Children race from school to child care to after-school athletics to church or synagogue to being dragged to the store with Mom or Dad. They need the security of traditions they can count on. They need to know that at the end of these wild days, there are moments at home that are predictable, restful, and pleasurable. These traditions can include:
- having a snack at the kitchen table and chatting about the day while a parent gets dinner
- family reading time just before bed
- morning rituals that are used as family send-offs. (Remember the famous "Hill Street Blues" send-off after the morning briefing? "Be careful out there!")
- popcorn and a video on Saturday night

- going to sleep to tapes of stories or good music in a variety of styles.

2. *Children need the help of traditions in order to slow down and reflect.* The rituals mentioned above, and others, not only provide stability but they also help children to slow down and reflect. Add to these the value of journal writing, library visits, time with crafts or hobbies, pen pals, and religious events.

3. *Children need rituals to add zest to life, just as the adult does.* It's important to have something to look forward to, no matter how simple it is. It's fun to look forward to Dad's pancakes on Sunday morning or hamburgers at McDonald's after the hockey game. Traditional or ritual activities or routines provide an assurance that the family will go on in spite of minor crises or the busyness we feel at times. They provide a sense of order and predictability, but just as important, they make a day special.

4. *Rituals help children remember to carry out their responsibilities.* Saturday rituals may be a way to get chores done. Don't underestimate the power of a repeated schedule for helping children to learn about responsible work. It helps to be able to say, "Our family always cleans the playroom on Saturday morning!" In our home, Saturday always included the bookkeeping and clean-up involved with four paper routes!

5. *Rituals and traditions provide a way to pass on our values.* If you read together nightly, your child soon knows that you value books. If you eat together and have a good talk as you do, the child learns something about togetherness and communication. If you have a weekly family council, the child learns (if you handle it right) that you value the opinions of others and the democratic process. If you celebrate religious holidays in some special way, the child learns the values that your faith provides. If you choose to spend your money in certain ways, the child learns what you value and the role

of money in those values. Our boys were taught that the paper route earnings had to be divided between their tithe to the church, their savings, and their spending. They still laughingly look at their birthday checks and admonish each other, "Remember! Ten, twenty, seventy!"

Working at Traditions

Some rituals and traditions are meaningful only if you put effort into them. The effort may be as simple as faithfully setting aside the necessary time. Or it may mean each family member taking responsibility for carrying out some piece of the special plans. Christmas and Hanukkah traditions often involve some special activity each day. They are far more meaningful when each family member participates. While there is a magic about things that are done *for* us, many of the most memorable events for a child are those they have fully participated in. Helping to plan and carry out the holiday gives a sense of competence, responsibility, and ownership.

If the aim is to transmit religious teachings and values, remember that children learn best by *doing*!

Changing Traditions

Rituals and traditions may need to change with time. As the children grow older, family times must be scheduled around dates and school social or athletic events. Rituals can provide reassurance if we move to a new neighborhood, but adaptations may be required for the new locale. Our interests may change with time, too. There is a difference between the repetition of a meaningful activity and rigidly repeating something that is no longer enjoyable or meaningful. Certainly, empty rituals should go! Periodically, it's a good idea to review family rituals and revise them if they need it.

What rituals and traditions does your family share?

Think about these possibilities:
- religious rituals
- seasonal rituals (sledding, hunting, camping, etc.)
- holiday rituals (besides religious holidays there are Fourth of July picnics, Labor Day trips, etc.)
- mealtime rituals (Sunday in the dining room, Friday the kids cook, etc.)
- bedtime rituals
- affectionate rituals (special code words for love, a back rub at bedtime, etc.)
- social and entertainment rituals.

As our family gathers for the holidays, one of our nicest traditions is the time spent remembering the traditions of past years. Families build people and people have memories. One of the joys of being human is the ability to build a storehouse of memories to sustain us. Remember the hostage crisis in Iran that began in 1979 and lasted over a year? After their release, some hostages recounted how they were sustained through their long captivity by recalling over and over the things they had done with family and friends: the rituals, the traditions, the stored memories.

During the months of joyous holidays, and during the more humdrum months that follow, think about the worth of the deposits you are making in your family memory banks. Plan now for rituals and traditions that will make your memories and those of your children worth remembering!

The Thinking Parent's Summary for Action

The thinking parent will plan for family rituals and traditions because:

1. Rituals and traditions provide predictability, stability, and personal comfort.
2. Rituals and traditions help the family slow down and enjoy each other and their world.
3. Rituals and traditions give the family something to look forward to.
4. Rituals and traditions help the family to carry out their responsibilities.
5. Rituals and traditions help the family to pass on their values.

The thinking parent will remember that rituals and traditions do not always revolve around big events. Some of the best traditions are related to the very ordinary ways we spend our days.

8

THE ART OF ASKING QUESTIONS

"Talk To Me! I'll Listen!"

- "My son won't talk to me!"
- "I can't find out anything about what goes on in school!"
- "He never thinks about anything!"
- "If she has an opinion, she hasn't shared it with me!"
- "What's with her? She's in a mood that's pure swamp water!"

Of course, no tricks or formulas can cure all of this. As a parent, you are doomed to being trapped under the "cone of silence." But if this sounds like your house, you might want to think about how you and your child talk together.

How to Ask Questions

Questions come in all sizes and shapes. The way you ask a question makes a lot of difference in how well you and your child communicate. Questions can be ranked on a sort of ladder, working from those that require the least thinking to those that require the most. Decide what you want to know and how involved you want the conversation to be. Then figure out which kind of question is most apt to get the right response. Your questions might be in one of the following categories:

1. *Trivial Pursuit: the shopping-list category of questions.* "What did you do in school today?" is too easy. All the child has to do is make a list. Even if your child answers you, you'll want more of an answer than, "I had math and went to the media center and did art and had yukky reading." But this kind of conversation is better than:

"Where did you go?"

"Out!"

"What did you do?"

"Nothing!"

Yes, it's too easy.

Some experts think children live so much in the present tense, "right this minute," that they really can't remember what happened a few hours ago. Unless something unusual happened, they really don't remember much about the day. If "something unusual" happened...? What do children consider unusual? The principal shaved his head and everybody wore their clothes backwards? Unfortunately, what the child considers important might not catch your attention. For example: "Kristina dropped her lunch tray right in front of Rob!"

Do you ignore that and go on to more interesting adult talk? (To find out, read on!) Shopping-list questions only require a child to *recall* a list of memorized facts or events. If you want more, you'll have to ask a more complicated question.

2. *Oprah, the Interviewer, category of questions.* If you listened, after all, to the bit of trivia that your child considered important, you might actually get an insight into the day.

This is information your child considered important. It might be the door to a whole discussion.
- "Did Kristina's lunch tray make a mess?"
- "What did Rob do?"

Your child is asked for *descriptions* and *results*. You are one step beyond the simple recall list. Good! You're getting deeper.
- "Why was reading yukky?"
- "How did you feel about that?"
- "Why did you do that?"

These questions make the child give *reasons* and *reactions*. But you need to be careful not to put the words into their mouths. "Did you feel good about that?" gives your child part of the answer. You've put words in his (her) mouth so that the answer is a too-easy "Yes." You can almost hear the television interviewer asking the guest to tell the audience how he (she) felt and why. Good interview skills can help parents.

3. *Perry Mason, the Detective, category of questions.* "If your teacher thought your worksheet wasn't good enough, what do you think he (she) expected you to do instead?" You're asking the child to look at all the clues and put together a theory about who or what killed the worksheet. What information did the teacher give? What did he (she) really want the child to do? You've asked your child to do some real thinking; he (she) will have to probe around.

This is a kind of cut and paste puzzle, moving the parts around until the solution or idea seems right. What the child is doing is called *synthesizing*.

"When Billy acted like that last week, there must have been something wrong. What do you think is happening with him?"

Your child will have to dig into what she knows about social and moral behavior. If she has ever experienced the same thing, she will compare Billy's behavior to her own experiences. She will put together her own theory about Billy's behavior. Like a good detective, she puts the clues together. It makes for a good discussion.

4. *Judge Wapner Presiding: the judgment and evaluation category of questions.* When you ask, "Which of your ideas is best?" you're asking for a judgment call. Your child is thinking up ideas for making up the poor work on the reading worksheet. Are you going to drop it with just a brainstormed list? Don't you want your child to solve the problem? She can't leave the courtroom without having a decision on the case.

Fine! Then which idea does she like best? Which idea is she interested in? Which idea will she work on? This requires your child to do some *evaluating*.

- "Your vote is for the poster idea! So ordered! Ask Dad to get you some posterboard!"
- "What do you think of Billy's behavior? What might happen because of this? What can you do about it?"

Your child is being asked to discuss the consequences of an action. When children are asked for *judgments, alternative plans,* and some ideas about possible *consequences,* they are thinking three steps deeper than the original simple recall question. Of course, Judge Wapner's word is law and you may only be looking for suggestions, but discussions like this can actually be exciting!

5. *Disneyland Imagineering: the creative "What if..." category of questions.* Questions that require imagination are the most fun of all: "If you could____, what would you do?" There are no right or wrong answers. People must think and use the creative side of their brains. These are called *open-ended questions* because there is no limit to what the answers can be:

"Let's pretend there is a store where there are bins and boxes full of spare people-parts. You go shopping for all the pieces to build a friend. What kind of parts would you get and what kind of friend would you build?"

Can't you just see a Disney audio-animatronic design being created? You'll have fun, but you'll also learn about the child's values related to friendship.

In short, when we talk with children, we often ask only simple recall questions. We don't get much of an answer because we haven't asked much of a question. We need to be ready to take the questions into deeper and deeper territory, questions that require more and more thinking.

How to Listen for Your Cue

1. Sometimes when we talk with children, we cut off all possibility of going deeper because we think we know the right answer. These answers cut off discussion:
- "Why did the teacher think my work was bad?"
  "Because you never think. You just race right through it!"
- "Why doesn't Billy like me?"
  "Don't be silly! Of course he likes you!"

When children ask *us* questions, we should think about the five levels of questioning and give more than a thoughtless and simplistic answer. We can respond with a question that will make him (her) reason.
- "Why are teachers mean?" Do you want to answer, "Teachers aren't mean"? If you do, you've closed the conversation.
- Instead, play Oprah the Interviewer and ask, "What makes you think teachers are mean?" Get the children to describe what happened and to come up with theories about why it happened.

Play Perry Mason, the Detective, and see if they can come up with ideas to make it better. Look for creative ideas, as a Disney Imagineer would.

If you want to have meaningful conversations with children, it's important to model that kind of discussion when they ask *us* questions. Pat answers squelch discussion.

2. *Tell your child about your day.* Be enthusiastic so your child will learn about enthusiastic discussions. If things didn't go too well at work, ask your child for an opinion.

3. *Talk about things besides school.* Try finding news items to discuss. Look for human interest stories in the paper or on television. Identify and describe world leaders. Look up the location of their countries with your child.

4. *Talk about your child's friends.* Discuss why they are special, their hobbies and why they enjoy them, the things they like to do together.

5. *Talk about hopes, dreams, and plans.* Share your own dreams with your child. Encourage your child to hope and dream, too.

Too often children don't talk with us because we don't talk with them. We talk *at* them. We lecture, express our opinions, and put down their opinions. Children who are used to discussing issues at home do better at thinking through problems at school. They learn to listen to the opinions of others and to evaluate them.

What questions have you asked today?
- "Did you do your homework?"
- "Did you hang up your clothes?"
- "Did you clean up the kitchen?"

Make a new list. Ask something that will get more of an answer. Get reacquainted with your child.

The Thinking Parent's Summary for Action

1. The thinking parent can encourage conversation with a child by asking the right kind of questions.

Trivial Pursuit questions are recall questions requiring only a list or a "yes" or "no."
- "What did you do today?"
- "Did you go to soccer?"

Oprah, the Interviewer, questions ask for descriptions, reasons, reactions, and results.
- "Why are you mad at John?"
- "What did your teacher like about your report?"
- "What did you think of that TV show?"

Perry Mason, the Detective, questions ask the child to examine the clues and come up with theories.
- "What makes the children act that way on the bus?"
- "Have you any ideas about what the school could do about that?"

Judge Wapner questions require evaluations and judgments followed by decisions for action.
- "What is the best way to sell the candy?" "Why?"
- "How can you carry that out?"
- "What will happen if you do it that way?"
- "Will people want to buy or will they just feel bothered?"

Disneyland Imagineering questions provide an opportunity to use pretend and creativity.
- "What would the world be like if people had no thumbs?"
- "What tools would have to be changed?"
- "What activities would you think would be difficult or impossible?"

2. The thinking parent needs to listen for cues.
   - Be careful about responses that cut off discussion.
   - Talk about your day in the ways you want to talk about your child's day.
   - Talk about something besides just school. Talk about friends, dreams, news, television programs, etc.
3. The thinking parent talks *with* a child, not *at* the child.

9

DISCIPLINE AND PUNISHMENT

"What Do I Expect?"

Whenever I ask parents what they want most to talk about, discipline (in one form or another) is high on the list. (Perhaps some day I will write a whole book on discipline.) Although discipline really involves all the other subjects in this volume, in this chapter I will pull together a few of the ideas parents have found directly helpful.

It is especially important to realize that I am an eclectic concerning discipline. I don't believe that just any method will do, but I also am very cautious when some publisher advertises in a slick ad that "this program will solve all your parenting problems." I know from experience that whatever you planned to do the next time your child left his bike in the drive will probably not work:

- because your child has just figured out a way to make you think it's all your fault
- because you can't remember what you planned
- because you just ran over the bike

- because this child is definitely different from his big brother and therefore is a mystery. (You probably brought the wrong baby home from the hospital!)

Children are different. Families are different. Parents need an armful of ideas and methods and they need to analyze when each will work and why. The main thing to remember is *not to choose a discipline technique simply because it will work in the short run.* Some very effective short-run methods may have terrible long-range effects. Spanking is one such method. It does work, but research tells about the lasting emotional scars from its use. Strict authoritarian parenting works, but many children raised this way suddenly do strange, anti-social, or unreasonable things as an outlet.

Positive Discipline Techniques: How to Choose Them

What is positive discipline? Discipline and punishment are not the same thing. Discipline is positive when:
- it defines limits
- it tells a child what he (she) can do. This includes the pep talks you give about chores or good behavior
- it includes listening when your child needs to talk about how much it hurts to be snubbed by a friend
- it includes all the preventive steps you take to help your child stay motivated and escape boredom
- it includes helping your child accept responsibility, act with honesty, and understand rules.
- it includes helping your child feel worthwhile.

To use positive discipline you will want to start with the following:

1. *Communicate with your child.* Communication is a two-

way street: driving in one direction, you talk and your *child* listens; driving in the other direction, your child talks and *you* listen. That should be easy! You've got so much to say about hanging up the towels and doing homework and cleaning rooms and no back-talk, but that's only one part of communicating. All you're doing is listing the rules and haranguing your child.

- Have you asked him (her) what is hard about the chores or the homework?
- Have you asked what will make them easier?
- Have you negotiated times and ideas for doing jobs better?

Communicating about the rules at home is based on having good communication in general. What do you really talk about?

- Do you talk about anything besides rules and expectations? What are your child's interests? Friends?
- What does your child dream about when it finally becomes quiet in the bedroom?
- Have you explained what your job is like, or how you feel about your own household chores?
- Have you read a book together or discussed a television show that you've watched together?

If you are used to talking about many things, discussion about the rules is easier. The bottom line is this: do you feel comfortable talking with your child? When all is said and done, we probably talk about very little besides our daily routine. If we are honest, this is probably true of our conversations with our spouse or partner as well as with our children.

"Where have you been?"
"Out!"
"What did you do?"
"Nothing!"

"Take out the garbage!"
"(Grunt!)"

2. Examine your rules and expectations. Think through the logic, fairness, and usefulness of the family rules. For example, your child is expected to do homework before going out to play. However, in the winter, it may get dark so early that by the time the homework is done it is too dark to go out. Should this be taken into consideration in setting the rules? Or, perhaps a certain rule was necessary and logical for one of your children, but for a second child who is more responsible and persistent it may be either unnecessary or communicate a lack of trust. Or perhaps the tasks involved have changed. Now that you have a dishwasher, which jobs are harder? The whole cleanup process may now be different.

Make sure the rules are clear; sometimes they aren't. When you tell your child to "clean up," he (she) may not understand what we consider clean. "But Mom, I threw out the moldy sandwich!" When you tell your child to "be nice to your sister," does that mean letting her play with a cherished toy, or... "But Dad, I stopped hitting her!"

Specifying exactly what you mean is one way to be sure you have communicated well with your child; it takes the guesswork out of following the rules.

Is the child old enough to do what you've asked? When you finally become specific about the separate steps and segments of your expectations, you may realize the child is not old enough to do certain parts of a task well. Bringing order out of a truly chaotic room may require more organizational skills than a second grader can muster. A third grader can make the sandwiches for lunch, but it may require more time than you thought. When you make a rule or state an expectation, be sure it is appropriate to your child's developmental age and stage.

Tell children what they are allowed to do. When they are

young, it's hard to tell them *not* to do a certain thing when they don't know what they *can* do in its place. Telling an active child not to run in the house makes it sound like you expect quiet and inactivity. What you want to add is "but you can run outside." When your child was a baby, you thought nothing of substituting a plastic cup for the breakable one in her hand. You were telling her what it was all right to do. Children in preschool and elementary years still need this assistance, which provides a more positive slant to rules.

Finally, it's important to decide if you are going to consistently enforce your rules, and which ones. If you sometimes allow your child to stay up later at night and sometimes do not, can you explain the variations in the rule to him? Under what conditions can he negotiate the rule? For example, can he always finish the game before you indicate it's time for bed? If so, what's to keep him from strategically starting a new game every night ten minutes before bedtime? If the rules are always arguable, then you will surely get arguments. Some rules may need to be flexible; some may require consistency.

Discuss your rules with your child. If you can't give him good reasons for a specific rule, it may not be a good rule.

3. Develop your child's thinking skills. By the time a child is an adolescent, we often look at behavior and wonder, "What in the world was she thinking of?" The ability to think through an action is partly developmental. A child needs to be old enough to hold several ideas in her head and, either mentally or on paper, put them in order and project what will happen if they are carried out. However, to a certain extent, this is also a skill we help children develop through careful questioning, discussion, and planning. By starting with the simpler problems of a young child, she can develop a habit of thinking "If I do this, what might happen?" Take the time to help the child ferret out the answers.

Part of the skill of thinking ahead is related to the child's independent behavior. Young children need to learn to choose activities and carry them out alone, entertaining themselves in acceptable ways. Also, your child learns that you will not always be on hand to solve problems. Encourage your child to make an effort to think about situations and create solutions. If their solutions are poor, then praise the willingness to try. Ask, "What would have been a better idea?" Your goal is to help your child develop decision-making skills that can be used when you aren't around.

Through all of this, your child will begin to understand that certain behaviors have certain consequences. Rather than preaching consequences at the child, try asking, "What do you think will happen if you do that?"

4. *Develop your child's self-esteem.* "Yes, honey, it was really lovely of you to bring me breakfast in bed!" (And scorch the teflon off the frying pan and scramble the shells with the eggs.) Or, "Next time you do it, you might want to fix toast and cereal, or, better yet, fix breakfast for Grandma." (Grandmothers think anything their grandchildren do is cute!)

Children who feel they are not lovable or capable are not going to be good problem solvers. They won't have the confidence to carry through their own ideas. This certainly does *not* mean giving false praise or praising poor ideas. (No! I don't think my grandchildren are cute all the time!) What you affirm is the *effort* (no matter what you are saying under your breath), while analyzing what other options are available. At some point (later on), the toast and cereal idea might be a good suggestion.

There is a big difference between lack of confidence and a realistic assessment of your own abilities. Children will always waver between being too timid to try and being sure they can conquer the world. Growing up is a process of finding a happy balance between the two extremes.

5. *Act.* Good discipline is extremely active. Don't wait un-

til the pillows have burst and there are feathers all over the room. Anticipate the probability. If the children continue this rowdy behavior, what will happen? Stop the action before the feathers fly! We all have a tendency to sit exhausted in our easy chair and yell:

"What are you children doing? Quiet down up there!"

"Did you guys hear me?"

"What was that crash?" (Still in easy chair, but voice getting more shrill.)

(Shriek!)

To act immediately before the children are completely out of control may be hard, but it's much easier than letting the behavior go haywire. Offer other choices while you are still calm enough to do so. Rechannel the activity before you really lose your cool!

If these ideas about discipline are new to you, read these pages again and think about how positive discipline should be. Think about how much real learning is involved. When deciding on a discipline technique, check it against the points mentioned in this chapter.

A Thinking Parent's Summary for Action

Positive discipline requires that you do these things:

1. Communicate with your child.
   - Think through what to say, how much to say, and when to stop talking.
   - Think of ways to truly listen.
   - Learn what to talk about in order to truly get to know your child.
2. Examine your rules and expectations.
   - Think through the logic, fairness, and usefulness of the family rules.
   - Think about whether or not a rule is clear.
   - Is the rule appropriate to your child's age and developmental stage?

- What is the actual meaning of the rule? Does it somehow include what the child can or should do and describe acceptable behavior? Does it go beyond "Don't"?
- Can you always (or almost always) enforce this rule? If it has too many exceptions, it needs rethinking.
- When you have thought the rules and expectations in the ways suggested, then discuss them with your child.

3. Develop your child's thinking skills.
   - Help your child to develop creative and responsible independence.
   - Help your child to plan ahead. Disciplined behavior grows from an understanding of what might happen next.
   - Help your child to think through the consequences of an act.
   - Help your child learn to entertain himself (herself), using time well and solving problems alone.
   - Learn to be a teacher and resource person to your child without doing all the thinking.

4. Develop your child's self-esteem.
   - Help your child to feel lovable and capable. Think through the ways you let your child know that he (she) is special and loved.
   - Analyze the ways you encourage your child to improve while you are affirming every success.
   - Help your child to set reasonable goals that show a confidence in self and an understanding of self.

5. Act.
   - Act immediately.

- Act before things get out of hand; act before you need to punish.
- Act to intercept or rechannel bad behavior.
- Act to offer better choices.

Punishment

Punishment will be discussed only enough to help you see how it differs from positive discipline. The rest of this chapter won't try to cover all that might be said about it.

What is punishment? It includes the steps a parent must take when positive discipline fails. We punish a child when:
- the disciplinary limits have been overstepped
- the child hasn't had enough self-confidence to say "no" to the gang
- they understood but ignored the rules.

Sometimes the breakdowns in discipline are partly the parent's fault. For example:
- The rule was not clear or age appropriate.
- The parent didn't listen or misinterpreted what was going on.
- The child had to misbehave to get the parent's attention.
- The parent was so autocratic that the child rebelled against an unreasonable rule in a situation where he (she) felt powerless.

The following steps are to help you consider how and when to punish.

1. Act. The rule of discipline—act before punishment becomes necessary—is also the first rule of punishment: don't put off the consequences when a child has misbehaved. Sometimes you really can't do anything immediately. However, you can at least:
- state what you really expected and what the child did that was wrong

- share your feelings about it
- get the child to express how he (she) feels
- set a time for discussion, negotiation, and development of the consequences.

Don't assume that you are doing your child a favor by ignoring misbehavior. She (he) might interpret your failure to act as an indication that this whole thing isn't very important anyway. Act so that your child will know you value the rules. Also, you aren't helping by ignoring behavior one time and exploding over the same behavior at another time. Act so that your child will know what to expect when he (she) behaves in that particular way again.

2. Set consequences. Choosing a natural or logical consequence is one approach to punishment. This means choosing a consequence that is directly related to the misbehavior. For example:

- If a child is late for dinner, there is nothing to eat.
- Losing Dad's hammer means earning and saving the money to replace it.
- Failing a test means less time watching television and using the time to study.

The consequences should matter to your child in some way. If he (she) is late for dinner because of a stop at the pizza place, missing dinner really doesn't matter. The consequence must be logically worked out in some other way. If the child is replacing the hammer and has no concept of the value of money, then there must be a way to help the child understand this. For example, you may need to explain that this is worth "three action figures."

Think before you speak! Set consequences you can and will carry out. If carrying out the threat will endanger your own sanity, you'd better think twice! Be prepared to carry out your threats—or don't mention them.

Be reasonable in setting the length of time that the consequence will be in effect. After a while a child forgets about his (her) misbehavior and sees the punishment as child abuse. It's very difficult to decide the length of time required for a punishment "to take." Part of this decision is based on the next point, the willingness of the child to mend the situation.

Consider whether there are ways your child can mend the situation and regain your confidence. Discuss them with the child. If he (she) wants to make something "right" again, the entire effort is much more positive. It emphasizes the "right" behavior instead of the "wrong" behavior. It helps the child learn the meaning of trust. It often requires as much time as the punishment might have taken.

3. Loss of privileges. This is a variation of the "consequences" method of punishment. A consequence is chosen that isn't natural or logical, but simply a way of enforcing the rule by taking away something meaningful to the child. Isolation or "grounding" are forms of losing privileges. Younger children find isolation difficult. For most punishment (except just "cooling off"), they need to be isolated in a place that isn't a pleasant playroom. Older children are "grounded," so they cannot join friends in activities they enjoy. For the "gang" age, this is real punishment.

Be careful what you say! You must be able to live with it. Sometimes it will be very hard to carry out the punishment, but it will be worth the effort. However, try to foresee if you will be punishing yourself more than the child.

To deny a privilege, choose from among those that are your child's favorites, things the child would like to own or places he (she) would like to go. It does no good to deny something the child doesn't care much about or even to deny something that wasn't counted on anyway.

Choose to deny a privilege that holds about the same weight in importance to the child as the seriousness of the offense. Every offense is not equally ground-shaking.

Be sure that the punishment is not always the same. It will lose its effectiveness.

4. *Choosing your own consequences.* When a parent can think ahead enough to outline a child's choices—before uncontrollable anger sets in—this method can make discipline and punishment very calm. The steps are:
- Note that a problem is about to "bloom."
- Think about the available choices and consequences. For example: "You can clean your room and then go to the movie, or you can spend the afternoon in the house. It's your choice!"
- State the choices calmly before the situation is out of hand.
- Do not nag or keep repeating the choices. Bite your tongue! Forget the old scenario:
(Loud!) "I told you to clean your room!"
(Louder!) "Your room still looks like the end of the world!"
(Ear splitting!) "Clean up now!"
- Instead, when the time has come, simply state what has happened: "I see you chose to stay home today!" The child learns that this was his (her) own choice and that he (she) alone is responsible for what has happened.
- Do not end with a moral lecture. You can discuss it later in simple terms if the child is ready to do so. When you do discuss it, let your child come up with the thoughts about what has been learned. "What happened here?" "What kept you from doing the cleaning?" "Did you really want to go to the movie? Then what should you have done?"

These ideas are only a few of the many approaches to discipline and punishment. (Among those not mentioned is the proper use of rewards.)

If you *must* punish, include positive steps to rebuild confidence, responsibility, communication, and love. Talk with your child about the next step. Always plan for ways to rebuild relationships. Always end in love!

- "What can we do to keep this from happening again?"
- "How can we make this a better rule?"
- "I know you have lots of good ideas. Can you think of something you might have done instead?"
- "It makes me unhappy when you behave like that. I love you, but I don't like that behavior!"

No parent is perfect! No child is perfect! You will often do things you regret. The most important thing you can do is to think ahead so that your behavior will be reasonable, suited to the child, and help her (him) to grow and learn. Begin with *positive discipline;* you will need far less punishment if you do.

The Thinking Parent's Summary for Action

When you must punish, consider the following:

1. Act.
   - Act immediately.
   - State what you really expected and what your child did that was wrong.
   - Share your feelings about it.
   - Get your child to tell how he (she) feels.
   - Set a time for discussion, negotiation, and development of the consequences.
2. Set consequences.
   - Choose a natural or a logical consequence.
   - The consequences should matter to your child.
   - Think before you speak! Set consequences you can and will carry out.
   - Be reasonable in setting the length of time the consequence will be in effect.

- Consider whether there are ways your child can mend the situation, regaining your confidence.
3. Set loss of privileges.
    - A consequence is chosen that is a way of enforcing the rule but isn't natural or logical.
    - Isolation or "grounding" are forms of losing privileges.
    - **Be careful what you say! You must be able to live with it.**
    - To deny a privilege, choose something that really matters to your child.
    - Match the importance of the privilege that is being denied to the importance of the offense.
    - Be sure that the punishment is not always the same; it will lose its effectiveness.
4. Choose your own consequences.
    - Note that a problem is about to "bloom."
    - Act before you get angry.
    - Think about the available choices and consequences. One choice offers compliance with your request; the other choice outlines the consequence of not complying.
    - State the choices to the child calmly.
    - Do not nag or keep repeating the choices.
    - When the time has come, simply state what has happened. "I see you chose....!"
    - Do not end with a moral lecture.
5. Always end in love!

10

TAKING TIME

Is It Quality Time or Everydailyness?

Time! If I had three wishes, one would be for "enough time." My husband and I have four grown sons. As we look back, we wonder if we gave them enough time. Of course, one way to look at that question would be to analyze how much of the time spent was "quality time." I'm not sure I want to do that, not because I'm afraid of what I might find, but because I don't know if there *is* such a thing!

George Rekers, a family therapist, uses a story about a steak dinner to make clear the relationship between quality and quantity. He asks that you imagine you've gone to a new gourmet restaurant and that you decide to treat yourself to their best steak even though it costs $18. The steak arrives on an expensive china plate, served with a flair by an impeccably dressed waiter. You note with shock and dismay that the steak is a one inch cube. In horror, you question the waiter, who assures you that quality is what counts and that this steak is *the best*. But if you're very hungry, you know that quantity also counts.*

---

*Quoted by Nick Stinnett and John Defrain in *Secrets of Strong Families* (New York: Berkley Books, 1986), p. 83.

As a family, we had lots of quality time: camping trips that lasted four or five weeks each and covered all 48 of the continental United States. Now that's a *real* test of family togetherness! I'm not sure, however, if all four sons would agree that those trips were the most memorable part of their upbringing. The boys turned their four-wheeled jail into the human equivalent of a hamster cage. I regretfully also acknowledge that hiking, rafting, or sightseeing aren't everyone's "cup of tea." Now that they are grown, the boys tell lots of other stories from their childhoods, many of which are a surprise to us, triggering long-forgotten memories of small happenings. Building "what-a-hut" in the back yard or cutting our own Christmas tree in the Florida woods took equal billing with four weeks on the road.

Have you ever planned a wonderful trip to the mountains and all that the children remember was the neat automatic faucets in the highway rest stop? You planned an educational day at the children's museum, and what was remembered was Johnny losing his mitten. You want to spend time one evening a week playing family games and the girls say they're "bored with Monopoly" and want to rent a cassette of *Halloween 13*.

On the other hand, have you ever noticed that the most wonderful time you spent with your child all week was the *unexpected* time, the time you didn't expect to spend with him (her)?

- Brad comes home with a picture he drew and wants to show it to you right away. In a moment of inspired grace you forget to say you are too busy right now. (You really are too tired from your busy day to even go to the kitchen to defrost the dinner.) You manage somehow to smile, sit still, and invite your young artist onto your lap with his picture. For five full minutes he tells you all about how he drew and revised his work of art. He suggests where it should

be displayed and cherishes your exhausted hug. Want to bet that in some way he will remember that time long after you have forgotten it?
- You are cleaning up the dinner dishes. Cheryl has a problem with her best friend. It doesn't take long for her to unburden the whole problem as you work together. Should she still call Betty her best friend when Betty has hurt her feelings so very much? As you work and talk, you are busy doing that wonderful double-duty that all parents should get used to. You are being the family manager and, at the same time, the family counselor. And Cheryl will remember that you were there for her when she needed you.

I remember vividly some time tidbits that my family spent with me as a child. I remember my dad, a pretty good mathematician, on his hands and knees with me trying to mathematically figure a way to match the plaids in a skirt I was making. It was the day and age of all-around pleats, and making them come out right was a real challenge. I remember my mom sitting with me as I lounged in the tub and told her all about my day. I remember watching my handyman dad fix things. I remember my librarian aunt teaching me to stamp book return slips. These memories have a sense of quality about them. They are stronger than the memories of some of the trips we took together. My parents are now dead. I wonder if they ever knew how much those bits of time meant to me.

- How about your memories?
- What stands out as quality time for you?

One insight I have about time is that time spent in a *strong family* is what counts. Life cannot be easily sifted to separate the quality bits from the disastrous moments. In fact, some disastrous moments are such strong learning situations that they become high quality time. The reality of life is that we often don't know until much later, until long after an event or an incident, that we have experienced something unforgettable and positive. In between the landmark events, life is so very "daily." That ability to make the most of everyday interactions is what makes time spent living together in a strong family into quality time.

Those Time Tidbits

When I think about all the unexpected time tidbits that make up our child-rearing time, I'm tempted to say that what comes first is our ability to "clean up" those little moments with the kids; then what follows is a stronger family. Here are some "time" suggestions that might help you enrich your time with your child:

- If there is more than one child, spend a little time each night with a different child. In two-parent families, alternate the parent, too.
- Think up ways to use the time you spend together in the car, in doctors' waiting rooms, etc. Come up with strings of word games or riddles, things to look for, or stories to tell. Put a tape in the car stereo and have a sing-along.
- Start a family journal. Each child has a day (or a week) for which he (she) is responsible. Each parent also takes a turn. Record a thought, a joy, an experience, a conversation, or a concern that stands out for that day (or week). Younger children can take their turns by drawing pictures. Occasionally read the journal out loud.
- Take a walk together around the block before dinner. No one needs to talk. It can just be a quiet unwinding time—a ritual.
- Use the dishwashing, vacuuming, yard-raking, chore-doing times as time together. That doesn't mean compulsive talking. Just enjoy the satisfaction of completing a job together.

- Read together. Try one chapter of a story a night. Perhaps the child's teacher or the librarian will suggest a book.
- Have a bedtime snack together. Make it a ritual.
- Watch a favorite television show together. Do it sitting close together, enjoying being near each other.
- Bake or cook together.
- Find some quick ritual that can be part of the morning goodbyes. Maybe a love note or joke can be tucked in the lunch box (or even your spouse's lunch box or brief case). Maybe it's just a special hug that's needed. (Remember the way the Sergeant on "Hill Street Blues" always ended the briefing: "Be careful out there!") In similar fashion, try some special phrase like "Knock 'em dead, Tiger!"
- Let your child overhear you saying something nice about him (her) to the neighbors, your spouse, or to another child.
- Work harder at making shopping trips more fun. If the children must go with you and the errands are necessities like getting groceries, try splitting up responsibilities with the children. One gets the milk, one gets the cereal, etc. Talk about your favorite things while you shop.

Quality time will always include those bigger or more complex events that we plan with family members: birthday or family parties; trips to zoos, museums, athletic events; family trips to other parts of the country. In our busy lives we must plan these events and mark them on our calendars, or else they will never happen. We look forward to these special times and they may, or may not, be memorable.

So is there such a thing as quality time? Yes, but each family member may define it differently. And don't be surprised if in the distant future, when all your children are grown, they list as quality time some tiny events you don't even recall. Realize that *quality time is a part of that quantity of everyday moments.*

> ### The Thinking Parent's Summary for Action
> The thinking parent remembers that quality time tidbits include:
> - talking, solving problems, sharing feelings
> - loving gestures and touching
> - companionable silence
> - family chores done together without quarreling
> - time in the car enroute to jobs or school, etc.
> - family rituals at bedtime, mealtime, weekends, start of the day
> - shared hobbies, games, projects
> - creative planning together
> - shared family stories, singing, joking, walking, biking.

11

Your Parenting Style

"What Kind of Parent Am I?"

- Today I said, "I don't care what you think! The answer is no!"
Yesterday I said, "Well, it might be okay just this once. Let's talk about it."
- Today I said, "Go figure out what you want to eat! I'm too tired to care!"
Yesterday I said, "The rule is no snacks after 4:00! I don't care how hungry you and your friend are!"

What kind of parent am I? One day I'm so strict, so unreasonable. The next day I'm really democratic. Sometimes I just don't give a hang! What kind of parent should I be?

Parenting is made up of numerous little skills and hundreds of everyday actions with, and reactions to, our children and their behavior. No one can tell you what kind of parent you should be. That can, and should, vary from family to family. The way you parent—the way you react in specific situations—is a result of a number of things, including:

- the way you were raised

- your personal and family values
- your personality
- your stress level
- your family schedule
- the personalities of your children.

There are, however, some general guidelines to parenting that may help you.

To begin, remember what I've already pointed out: there is no such thing as perfect parenting. Probably it's a good thing that there are no perfect parents. Perfect parents and perfect children would likely have a terrible time adjusting to an imperfect world.

Let's look at how you were raised. You may not have always thought your parents were great. As children, you probably yelled:

- "Wait till I have kids! I won't treat them like that!"
- "You're mean! I'll never be mean to my kids!"

Then today you heard for the umpteenth time about how Susie's mother lets her wear lipstick and you heard yourself shouting, "I never wore lipstick until I was in eighth grade and neither will you!" (Great heavens! I sound just like my mother!) "No! You can't have money for a CD! When I was a kid I had a paper route and I earned every penny for my luxuries!" (Great heavens! I sound just like my father!)

Some of your parenting is a reaction to the way you were raised. You resented the physical punishment you received and you vowed never to do that to your own children. And you may have kept that promise to yourself. In fact, you may have swung the other way and not be disciplining at all because you don't know what the other options are.

Three Styles of Parenting

Let's look at three parenting styles that have been identified by family researchers. It may help you identify where you stand in terms of philosophy and method. Many years ago

Diana Baumrind contrasted three groups of children and described the child-rearing practices of their parents.

1. *Authoritarian Parents.* "Parents of children who, relative to the others, were discontented, withdrawn, and distrustful, were themselves detached and controlling, and somewhat less warm than the other parents. These may be called authoritarian parents." *

Parents like this believe that child-rearing is like a war. The children are out to get you and you'd better keep control at all costs. Children respect power. "Talk to my old man? No way! I just keep clear in case he is in a bad mood! Mom is always saying, 'Play outside! Daddy's had a hard day!'" This is also the cold mother figure of Angela Channing in TV's *Falcon Crest* in the 1980s.

Authoritarian parents have a set standard of conduct. They value obedience above all else. Verbal give and take is not encouraged. Reasons for rules aren't needed because rules are rules... and the rule is right. Furthermore, the parent is always right.

2. *Authoritative Parents* (not authoritarian). "Parents of children who were the most self-reliant, self-controlled, explorative and content were themselves controlling and demanding: but they were also warm, rational, and receptive to the child's communication. This unique combination of high control and positive encouragement of the child's autonomous and independent strivings can be called authoritative parental behavior." *

This kind of parent is a bit like Bill Cosby's Dr. Huxtable on television. Cosby was probably more to the controlling side than some authoritative parents and his warmth was wrapped up in his "TV humor," but the idea is there. (Remember that this word is "authoritative." Don't confuse

---

* *The Young Child: Reviews of Research*, Vol. 2, Willard Hartup, ed., Washington, D.C., National Association for the Education of Young Children, 1972, pp. 202-24.

it with "authoritarian.") These parents encourage reasoning. They see themselves as the final authority, but children are free to negotiate the rules. Children are loved and encouraged, but are not allowed to trample on the rights of other family members.

In many places this kind of family is called democratic. This is a confusing term. In a democracy everyone is equal. In a family the parents should be "more equal" than the children and should have the final say. In general, the style falls in the "middle of the road."

3. *Permissive Parents.* "Parents of the least self-reliant, explorative, and self-controlled children were themselves non-controlling, non-demanding, and relatively warm. These can be called permissive parents." *

These parents are anxious to be a buddy, not a parent. They think parenting should be all fun and no rules. They are terribly concerned about whether their child likes them. As a result, they never set clear boundaries and are unable to teach clear decision making. They consult with the child as an equal on all decisions, including policy decisions. They see themselves as resources rather than authorities. Children regulate their own activities if they are regulated at all. The parent assumes that reasoning is all that is needed.

Discipline and Parenting Styles

How do the various parenting styles relate to discipline methods?

1. Authoritarian parents use rewards and punishment freely. Obey the rules and you get a reward. Disobey and you are punished. It's apt to be pretty black and white. Rules are, after all, vital. A child earns respect, praise, even love, because the rules are obeyed. If the child disobeys, the parent may

---

* *The Young Child: Reviews of Research,* Vol. 2, Willard Hartup, ed., Washington, D.C., National Association for the Education of Young Children, 1972, pp. 202-24.

yell or threaten and withdraw love. The authoritarian parent is afraid of losing power and afraid the child will somehow get the upper hand.

When an authoritarian parent tells a child the rules, statements are made as commands. "Listen to the teacher!" "Wash your hands!" "Don't yell!" All of us have to do a certain amount of such commanding. But somewhere along the line children need to have been taught the *reasons* for the commands or rules.

- "If you listen to the teacher, you'll be able to solve the problem."
- "Dirty hands can carry germs to your mouth and make you sick."
- "If everyone yells, we will all get tense and upset."

I'm not saying that it's always appropriate to be so wordy. But good discipline should *teach*. A child should know why a certain behavior is good or helpful.

2. *Authoritative parents teach their children the reasons behind the rules.* They then allow their children to learn by the consequences of their actions. If a child is always late for dinner, the natural consequence is that the child goes hungry. The child learns nothing from the parent who becomes a servant and prepares a special late meal. If a child gets up too late to catch the school bus each morning, the logical consequence is having to walk to school. Under certain circumstances this may not be practical but other logical consequences can then be devised. The child might have to stay home but stay in bed. The child might be forced to miss breakfast in order to make the bus—and so on. Authoritative parents negotiate rules, allowing the child to have input and compromising when practical or possible. But the authoritative parent has the final say!

Authoritative parents freely discuss the way a child's behavior makes the parent feel. The child is taught to care about the feelings of others. The parents show that they care about the feelings of the child. Therefore, they can expect the child to be anxious to live up to parental expectations. There is mutual respect.

3. *Permissive parents plead, hope, give up, and give in.* Somehow they feel an obligation to please the child. It is the permissive parent who fixes special meals for the chronically late child. The child demands—the parent does as commanded. Sometimes the parent becomes frustrated and clamps down. The resentful child cannot understand the inconsistency; the parent can't stand the child's back-talk and tunes the child out. The whole situation swings back and forth from a loving servant parent to a parent who suddenly screams and yells or else becomes silent and simply doesn't react at all. The child may never be really sure of the rules. The parent chooses all the easy ways out of situations.

Do you see yourself in one of these discipline styles? At times we all parent a little in all three styles. But which style is closest to the way you usually react? As is often the case, the middle-of-the-road style, research shows, produces the most self-disciplined, competent, resilient, spontaneous, and curious children. That style is seen best in the authoritative parent.

Within each of the three general parenting styles is a broad spectrum of ways to handle child-rearing issues. You can be an authoritative parent but appear very different in style from your neighbor who may also be authoritative. The variations will be caused by hundreds of differences in personality, family schedule, family interests and abilities, and family priorities. Let's look a bit more at the whole question of parental styles and influence.

Parenting Style and Goals

We know that being a perfect parent is an unreasonable goal. However, most of us hope that our children will do well in school, be liked by their teachers and peers, do their chores without being nagged, and think before they act. In short, we really want our children to be independent, responsible, and likeable, and not subservient or dependent. Often our goals change through the years, but the school years do trigger some of the first serious thinking about our goals. In order to help our children develop according to our goals, we form images of the kind of parent we want to be.

The image and goal of the authoritative parent is one of being in charge, but also of assuming that their children are responsible for their own behavior. For example, if your child fails to do her homework, it isn't (necessarily) your fault. It is hers! Your own worth as a parent and as a person is not necessarily involved. By "necessarily" I mean that I am assuming that the parent has provided the time, support, and materials needed for the child to do the homework. Beyond that, the child is responsible for actually doing it. The child's successes and failures are his—not yours!

Parenting Style and Your Child's Life

How involved in your child's life should you be? Deciding what is the right degree of involvement can be one of the hardest parts of parenting. There are hovering parents, neglectful parents, directive parents, unstructured parents, and more. If you are going to be authoritative, how involved are you?

John Rosemond, child psychologist and columnist, has taken the interesting concept of Management By Wandering Around and applied it to Parenting By Wandering Around.* The PBWA method of parenting means that you are certainly on hand and in charge. However, you aren't sitting down to do the child's homework for him or telling her how to do

---

* "Parents," John Rosemond, *St. Paul Pioneer Press*, March 15, 1986, Knight-Ridder News Service.

it so that creativity is squelched. In PBWA parenting, which is certainly authoritative, your child makes the mistakes and your child is the one who succeeds. His (her) accomplishments are not seen as a sign of the success or failure of your parenting style, but the child's attitudes and approach *are* a sign of the success or failure of your style.

Look again at the homework example. How involved should you be in your child's homework responsibilities? When dealing with the homework issue, parental involvement takes the form of:

- provision of time, materials, and a space to work
- encouragement
- monitoring
- concern for thinking skills rather than the number of right answers
- willingness to discuss the homework without doing the work or solving the problems.

So much of effective parenting means being there at the right time and both listening and discussing matters openly. The homework issue involves these same things.

Let me remind all parents that you are influencing your child, even when you aren't aware of it. You are involved in your child's life in many subtle ways. If you think that having your child away from home all day in school and after-school child care means that you no longer are influential in her (his) life, you are very wrong. Current research on child care services and their effects on children indicate that a child may spend ten hours a day in child care and still be influenced more by one hour with a parent. For better or worse, our children take us with them. The values and attitudes you have consciously or unconsciously taught your child will probably stick with them.

Ways We Influence Children

1. *The way you were parented influences the way you parent.* Do

you find yourself doing some of the same things your parents did to you? Do you find yourself saying, "I won't treat my child the way I was treated?" Sometimes, though, you still find yourself slipping into those old ways.

2. *Although you use many parenting skills and styles, you usually have a "favored" or dominant parenting style.* Research shows that there are great advantages to the middle-of-the-road authoritative style, which is warm, firm, and respectful of the rights of both parent and child.

3. *The backlog of all the early years you spent in child rearing, from birth to the present, influences your children for the rest of their lives, no matter where they are.*

4. *The love and attachment your child feels toward you as a parent has an effect.* On the positive side, this creeps into the child's desire to please you and get attention from you. On the negative side, this may show up in a desire to control you or seek revenge. But positive or negative, your child carries those feelings everywhere throughout life.

5. *There is another emotional side to involvement.* Your child learns from you the emotions that carry him (her) through the day. One researcher has found that parental irritability can be a corrosive factor. Small flare-ups by tired parents at the end of the day are normal. But the parent who *always* responds with a cross snappiness eats away at a child's emotional well-being. In fact, they also eat away at their own well-being and the well-being of their spouse. The way a parent handles anger and the way the child learns to handle anger influence the home atmosphere and overflow into the child's world with friends and at school.

The child who is able to see life as a positive and good challenge, who greets the new day with excitement and pleasure, who feels good about himself or herself probably has parents who feel that way too. These emotional influences, which the child carries from home out into the world, affect her (his) ability to think creatively and to solve problems effectively. It is vital that parents examine their parenting style in order to assess their emotional influence and involvement with their children.

6. *Influences on the child's thinking skills come from many sources.* One source is the discipline method you have used. Children need to have clear expectations gauged to their age and ability. They will feel more competent than children whose parents have always expected too much and have never been satisfied. We all know people who have said that they could never please their parents; they either gave up or carried that insecurity around for the rest of their lives.

The converse of this is the parent who doesn't expect enough. Permissive parents often fall into this category. The child is never challenged and doesn't need to think in order to produce.

Children who feel they have a right to negotiate the rules learn valuable skills for later life. They learn the reasons for the rules. They know how to present a case and how to follow through. They also learn that they may not always win. *Authoritative* parents are still in charge, but they know that children do need to win occasionally. *Authoritarian parents*, on the other hand, are so afraid of losing power that they fear negotiations, changes in rules, and failure to obey.

7. *The child brings from home a feeling of being a valuable person.* We are our child's most important fan club. It *is* possible to have too hovering and protective an approach to child rearing—but that is not the same as unconditional love for your child. Only you will ever love your child this much. Do it!

- You won't fight your child's battles, but you will love him.
- You won't say she is always right, but you will love her.
- You will sometimes be disgusted with behavior, but you will always love the child.

In summary, hovering parents may be authoritarian. They do not trust the child to think for herself. When the child is on his own, he isn't sure how to behave. The child is unsure about her own competence. Authoritarian parents may also be directive. It's easier to tell the child every move to make and expect unquestioning obedience than to explain "why" and teach "how."

Neglectful or unstructured parents may be permissive. They feel the child is able to make all his (her) decisions and that they will somehow stifle the child by making rules and monitoring behavior. The child never learns any reasons for rules and may not develop a concern for others.

Authoritative parents are firm, but also warm, open, and good listeners and negotiators. In order to choose authoritative techniques, it is important to examine a few of the ways our choice of parenting style influences our children. Included are the way the child views each day, the child's self-view, thinking skills, ability to handle anger, and reaction to discipline. Authoritative parents are aware of the way their style affects children and use their style as a teaching tool.

If you are trying to be an authoritative parent, you will make many mistakes, you will mix in bits of permissiveness and authoritarianism, you will sometimes feel great and sometimes feel guilty—but you will be open to your child and your child's world and, when you aren't too worn out, you will appreciate the parenting challenge that is yours.

The Thinking Parent's Summary for Action

Examine these three parenting styles:
- authoritarian
- authoritative
- permissive.

Of the three, authoritative parenting seems to produce the most self-reliant, self-controlled, and content children. Seriously consider the possibility of choosing this parenting style. To do so, you will want to:
- Examine your parenting goals. How do your goals fit with this parenting style? Balance your need to be in charge and your need to teach your children to be responsible for their own behavior.
- Examine your degree of involvement in your child's life. Realize that this involvement will affect your ability to be an authoritative parent.

You influence children by:
- the way you were parented
- the way you parented your child from birth on
- the kind of emotional attachment your child has to you
- the way you handle daily tensions, anger, and problems
- your expectations and attitude toward rules
- your unconditional love.

12

MOTIVATION TO LEARN

"My Kid Doesn't Want to Learn!"

What do you do when your child:
- won't try
- appears lazy
- seems immature
- probably has a poor self-concept
- is rebellious?

What will become of your child?
- Johnny is perfectly capable but never seems to complete his schoolwork. He does mediocre work on tests and really acts like he doesn't care.
- Kirsten keeps telling the teacher that the work is too hard and sometimes cries in school. Embarrassed, she then wisecracks and "acts up."

These are children whose parents and teachers are sure they have more ability than their schoolwork shows. They are "underachievers." At home they can remember all the detailed sports data and complex game rules; they can solve real-life problems once they are out of school. What has gone wrong?

Schoolwork and Real Work

One possible problem with underachievers, and with all children in school today, is being unable to see any connection with what they are doing now and what they will become. We are always asking children, "What do you want to do when you grow up?" How do you explain to a child the connections between current schoolwork and a vague desire to be a "computer worker" or an "artist" or an "electronics expert"?

Everything is more complex and technical today. Children have few chances to see just what is involved in the careers they might choose. Unless they are going to go into "the family business," they can only imagine the special courses of study in business, electronics, computers, nutrition, law, medicine, etc. It is hard for them to make a direct connection with what they are learning in school today.

Businesses say that our children are poorly prepared for work and they blame the schools. Actually, schools are in some ways better than they have ever been. The problem is that the workplace has changed and students must know different things to succeed. The result is that more people go to school for additional training. However, the students who don't go on and those who might have been dropouts years ago may not have the skills that businesses require.

To remedy this, schools and families need to start preparing the children when they are young. Elementary school children are in a stage that is referred to as the "stage of industry." They have much informal knowledge, small bits of unconnected information that they have picked up from television, friends, or curious observation. For example, no parent needs to be told that children's informal knowledge about sex is greater than ever before. Television and the print media are full of it. So, of course, these human sponges pick it up—whether it is accurate or not. The same is true of odd bits of technical information about sports, machines, Earth, the community, etc. Real learning involves *doing* something with this knowledge and, in this stage of industry, children *want* to do something. Parents and teachers often fail to build on what children already know and what they can and want to *do* with their knowledge.

When you have found something that captures the underachiever's attention, encourage the child to learn more about it. Successful people are often great "question askers"; they ask questions to find out "who to ask." If you want to know how to build shelves or a plant stand, you ask a carpenter friend or the shop teacher. They can refer you to others who know more specific answers. If you want to know about a specific computer problem, you try the teacher, an expert at a local computer store, or someone who teaches a community education class in the district. They can refer you to others. You can build a whole house yourself by knowing who to ask and by asking the right questions! Underachievers especially need to learn this skill of persistent question asking.

1. How can you help your child achieve?
    - Cooperate fully with your child's teacher. This will be hard work for all of you. Ask the teacher for weekly or bi-weekly periodic progress reports in which the child's homework, assignments, test scores, and behavior are included. This should be done with the cooperation of your child. Link progress to a system of small rewards or privileges.
    - Keep in touch with the teacher regularly regarding the weekly reports.
    - Ask the teacher if there are other parents with similar problems with whom you may be in contact. Idea sharing can be helpful.
    - Ask about other school services that might provide additional counseling or advice for you and your child.

2. What can you do to connect your child's interest to the real world?
- Ask your child to teach you about the game, hobby, or skill in which he (she) is interested. Whether it's a computer game, a sport, baseball cards, or something else, your child will gain a sense of power as a teacher. Also, your child will begin to see the role a teacher must fill.
- Let your child see you at work. Does your work interest him (her)? Explain it to the child, including what you like about it.
- Notice people at work or play using skills that your child might find interesting. Point this out to him (her).
- Help your child to have enough confidence to approach adults or other young people so they can get information.
- Encourage your child to ask questions. Help her (him) to learn how to phrase them so that they get answers. They can ask about games or hobbies or work skills.

Achievement and Self-Esteem

"I am lovable and capable...." Of what? Our generation of parents is truly concerned that their children have positive self-esteem. When asked to list their values or their dreams for their children, the parents inevitably include "high self-esteem." We send children home with buttons that say, "I am lovable and capable," but when you ask the child about the button, he (she) may be unable to tell you what he is "capable" of doing. Elementary school children still need concrete, tangible examples in order to understand. If they can't see the direct *results* of something at which they are "capable," then praising their competence is an empty exercise.

One of the theories about underachievers is that they

have low self-esteem. Some psychologists are beginning to dispute this. Delinquent teenage boys can have very high self-esteem. Members of a street gang who have been accused of killing a police officer may very well have high self-esteem. They may consider themselves "cool" and be held in high regard by their peers. Psychologist Hazel Marcus argues that a more revealing sign of adolescent's self-worth lies not in how good they feel about themselves, but in what they can envision for themselves in the future. People are guided by their "possible selves."

"Possible selves" may not be directly related to self-esteem, but may be better predictors of behavior according to psychologist Carole Tavris. While we want our children to feel they are lovable and capable, we also want them to know what they are capable of and to have dreams of how they will use that capability in the future.

So we have come full circle. Underachieving children need to be able to see how their skills today are relevant to their dreams for their future. They need to feel good about their capability of realizing those dreams.

What can you do to connect self-esteem with your child's "possible selves"?

- Build a feeling of trust and respect between you and your child.
- Encourage your child to try new things.
- Be patient with the process of teaching new skills to your child. Help him (her) feel the rewards of every gain; sometimes they are hard-earned gains.
- Help your child to risk learning new things. Risking sometimes means failing. Allow him (her) to risk and fail.
- Help your child learn from failures. Failures should not discourage him (her) to the point of giving up.
- Give honest feedback. Children will accept honest feedback from those they respect and trust. Some

feedback may be negative, some positive, but children need to learn to listen to it and act on it.
- Know your child's interests and strengths. What kind of facts does he (she) seem to remember? What games does your child play? How does your child seem to learn best?

Children who are underachievers pose perplexing problems for parents and teachers. It is most important that they see themselves as cooperative team members as they work on the problem. It is also important that community members and businesses that might be related to the child's interests be enlisted whenever possible to capture his (her) enthusiasm for learning.

These are important years! Try to recapture them!

The Thinking Parent's Summary for Action
To motivate children to learn and achieve:
1. Work with your child's teacher.
   - Find out what information would help you to understand what your child is learning. Use the information to keep track of his (her) progress.
   - Contact other parents with similar problems.
   - Look for school services providing tutoring or counseling.
2. Link your child's interests to the real world.
   - Let your child teach you a game, or hobby, or skill.
   - Let your child see you at work; talk with him (her) about it.
   - Point out people doing interesting jobs.
   - Help your child to learn to ask questions of people with skills that interest him (her).
3. Link your child's dreams of a future self with a growing self-esteem.
   - Build trust between yourself and your child.
   - Help your child risk new things and learn from success and failure.
   - Give honest feedback.
   - Notice your child's strengths and build on them.

13

BEGINNING A NEW SCHOOL YEAR

Resolutions

Most people think of January 1 as the time to make resolutions. For your school-age child, September 1 is New Year's Day, the beginning of a new school year and the beginning of a new year for you as a parent. What better time to make resolutions for the new school year!

This chapter is divided into two main sections: Part 1 deals with school-related resolutions, home-related resolutions, and resolutions to build character and self-discipline. These are examined from the parent's and from the child's points of view. Part 2 deals with resolutions related to self-esteem. These are also examined from both the parent's and the child's perspectives. These two parts go hand in hand; our actions and self-esteem are interdependent.

Part 1: General Actions
Resolutions for Parents
School-Related
1. I will talk with my child's teacher at least once each grad-

ing period, preferably in the early weeks of a grading period so there is still time for my child to improve.

2. I will go to parent conferences with a pencil and paper so I can write down the teacher's suggestions and make notes of the ideas we have both brainstormed for my child.

3. I will realize that I may know things about my child that could be helpful to the teacher. I will keep the teacher informed of these observations.

4. I will think of our home and the school as partners in the education of my child. I will assume that we are all aiming at cooperative concern for the benefit of my child.

5. I will attend the meetings of the parent-teacher organization and become interested in the concerns of all the parents of our school.

Home-Related
6. I will talk with my child. I will not talk just about disciplinary measures or household routines. I will talk with my child about his (her) feelings, hopes, dreams, friendships, and interests.

7. I will spend time with my child at least once a week. I will let my child help in choosing the activity we will share.

8. I will read to my child and with my child. If my child is older, I will get suggestions for a family (out loud) reading time from the children's librarian at our public library.

9. I will help my child set reasonable homework hours. We will work this out together.

10. I will set a healthy bedtime hour for my child.

11. I will see that my child gets a healthy breakfast each morning.

Character- and Discipline-Related
12. I will help my child learn decision-making skills. I will give him (her) appropriate opportunities to make decisions.

13. I will help my child learn responsibility by helping

her (him) to understand the consequences of actions. I will allow my child to experience consequences in all ways possible without unreasonably protecting him (her).

14. I will set firm limits, but I will not be inflexible and rigid. This means I will examine the family rules, and retain those I consider fair and reasonable. I will then be sure my child understands the rules.

15. In disciplinary situations, I will act *before* a situation has gone on long enough to make me angry and to make punishment necessary. I will redirect questionable behavior *immediately* before it gets out of hand.

16. I will avoid conflicts and quarrels as the day begins in our family so that my child will not go to school under stress.

17. I will not expect myself to be perfect—nor my child. I will learn to understand my moods.

Of course, there are many other good resolutions for the year. You undoubtedly can think of some that are unique to your own family situation. The number of resolutions can be overwhelming. However, most of these are not time-consuming. They are attitudes or habits. Consider them and try to make them part of your life.

Resolutions for Children

These resolutions are for your child. Sit down with your child and go over those that are appropriate before the school year gets any older.

School-Related

1. I will talk with my teacher about the expectations of the class. Each week, I will ask my teacher if I am doing what is expected.

2. I will learn what study habits are important to my teacher. If I don't know how to study in the ways she expects, I will ask her (him) for help.

3. I will learn the school rules.

4. I will take my schoolwork home and explain to my parent(s) what I am doing. I will not expect my parent(s) to do my homework for me. I will simply keep them informed.

5. I will set a time to do my homework and I will not let activities with my friends take the place of my homework time.

6. I will keep my parent(s) informed of school activities and invite them to participate in those that could or should involve parent(s).

Home-Related
7. I will lay out my school clothes, books, and other school-related equipment the night before. I will try to avoid having to rush around during the morning before school.

8. I will go to bed at the hour my parent(s) and I agree upon.

9. I will learn to set my alarm clock. I will get up in time to be cheerful (or at least polite) to my family.

10. I will not watch TV all the time. I will work out my TV schedule with my parent(s). We will decide on my TV daily (or weekly) limit.

11. I will read something for pleasure every day.

Character- and Discipline-Related
12. I will learn to think ahead. When I make a decision, I will think, "What will happen if I do this?" I will learn about the consequences of my actions.

13. I will learn the rules in my home. If I don't understand the rules, I will ask for reasons and explanations. When I understand the rules, I will take responsibility for following them.

14. I will always let my parent(s) know where I am going and how I can be reached.

15. I will learn to be a good friend. I will not try to buy

friendship with things or with bad behavior. If a friend expects me to do something I know is wrong, I will seriously think about whether that person is a good friend to have.

This list of resolutions is missing a vital part. Every home needs to think about ways they can bolster the self-esteem of each family member. Some research indicates that a high self-esteem may be more important than IQ in assuring your child's academic success.

Part 2: Self-Esteem

We can be what we believe ourselves to be. If we have been treated as valuable people, we will believe we are valuable. If we have been treated as capable people, we will believe we are capable.

We have talked about resolutions related to school, home activities, discipline, and character-building. Most of these are related to the self-esteem-building resolutions I suggest in this section. At the core of each human being is a picture we have painted of what and who and why we are. That picture, that self-image, may be more important than IQ in determining our level of achievement in life.

Included here, as in Part 1, are resolutions for both adults and children. Adults and children are very much alike in their need to feel loved and competent. The resolutions of Part 2, combined with those of Part 1, are the foundations on which to build a good school year, and even more, a good life.

Resolutions for Parents

The goal of each of these resolutions is a positive self-esteem for a capable, caring, and responsible child.

1. I will realize that my child's sense of self is a reflection of the way I feel about myself. In order to help my child have a positive self-esteem, I must work on having a positive feeling about my own self.

2. I will say three positive things about my child's character every day. This means I will think about who my child *is*—not just what my child does. I will talk about my child as honest, cheerful, thoughtful, friendly, persevering, creative, etc.

3. I will say three positive things about my child's efforts every day. These are the things my child *does*. They may not be total successes but they are the activities in which my child has made a genuine effort. I will always encourage, but I will not give false praise. My child will see through false praise and learn that my praise is not to be trusted. I will give my child:
- praise for effort
- assurance of love
- ways to improve.

4. I will tell my child how glad I am that he (she) is part of our family. I will do this every day. I will express my pleasure at having my child with me when I shop or work or read or watch television. I will be my child's Number 1 Fan Club! I will always love my child and not expect him (her) to earn my love.

5. I will thank my child for the kinds of things I would like to be thanked for. I will treat my child as a respected person deserving of courtesy.

6. I will encourage my child to talk about feelings, hopes, dreams, interests, and friendships. I will not be judgmental about the things he (she) shares with me.

7. I will avoid negative labels related to character. When my child misbehaves, I will not use labels like stupid, dumb, lazy, or thoughtless. I will only label *actions*. I will be sure my child understands he (she) is not a bad person, but a good person who has done a bad thing.

8. I will realize that my child's success is not the measure of my success as a person. When my child fails, I am not a failure, too. I am still a capable, worthwhile parent.

9. I will understand that my child is a unique human being. My child's job is to fulfill his (her) own potential—not my own personal dreams. He (she) will not be in drama club or on the soccer team because it was something I always wanted to do myself. My child will seek out talents and interests that are his (her) own. My child will set his (her) own goals.

10. I will not expect myself to be perfect—or my child either. I will learn to understand my moods, my stresses, and my energy cycle. I will not make impossible demands on myself or my child.

Other-Related
Our sense of who we are is built in our homes, schools, and communities. We begin to understand who we are when we see how we fit into the lives around us. If our relationships are positive, we become positive and confident. If our relationships are negative, we become insecure and hesitant. Parents are at least partially responsible for the ways these social relationships grow.

11. I will respect my child's privacy. Everyone needs times to be alone, to have their own space, their own thoughts.

12. I will understand that children have days when their energy is depleted, days when they feel stressed. I will learn the difference between the cues of stress that require understanding and the cues of misbehavior that might require punishment. I will learn to understand my child's moods.

13. I will not compare my child with other children in our family or with other children in the neighborhood, church, synagogue, or social group. I will treat my child as a unique individual.

14. I will try to do something unexpected and thoughtful for my child each week.

Resolutions for Children

1. Everyday I will tell myself that I am a worthwhile, capable, pleasant person. Then I will act that way. I will look for my own unique talents and style.

2. I will realize that I can make things happen. There will be many helpful people who will support me and help me make my dreams come true. I need to remember and be grateful to these people, but the most important efforts will be my own.

3. I will learn to set reasonable goals for myself and learn to work toward accomplishing those goals. I will not make impossible demands upon myself. If I need help in setting my goals, I will ask for it.

4. I will understand that growing up takes lots of personal effort and work.

5. I will learn that failure is not the end of everything. I will understand that I must risk trying new things—risk possible failure—in order to grow. I will evaluate my efforts and use them to learn better ways.

6. I will not expect myself to be perfect—or my parent(s). This understanding will be reflected in the goals I have chosen, the way I deal with success and failure, and in the way I treat my parent(s).

Other-Related

7. I will tell my parent(s) every day how much I love and appreciate them.

8. I will thank my parent(s) when they spend time with me or do things for me. I will not act as if my parent(s) are my personal servants, as if I have a constitutional right to be waited on. I will treat them with respect, just as I hope to be treated respectfully.

9. If I need time to talk or do things with my parents, I will learn to ask for it. No one can read my mind.

10. I will ask my parent(s) and teachers for suggestions. I

will not take these as personal attacks but as genuine efforts to help me improve.

11. I will realize that part of the family mood is my responsibility. I will learn to know when I'm tense or crabby. I will try to be cheerful.

12. I will be sensitive to the fact that adults (teachers and parents) have good and bad days just as I do.

13. I will not call my parent(s) names, just as I don't want them to call me names. I will believe that they do the best they can for me and set rules that are as wise as they can know. I will, therefore, do the best I can for them, too.

14. I will learn to talk with my parent(s) about something besides what's on TV and how to get a ride to my friend's house. I will talk about their thoughts and feelings, their childhood stories, their hopes and dreams.

15. I will learn to be a good friend. If a friend expects me to do things that I know are wrong, I will seriously think about whether that person is a good friend to have.

16. I will do something unexpected and thoughtful for someone else each week. I will not do it for a reward, but for the personal sense of satisfaction that comes from giving genuine service to someone else.

Sit down with your child and use the resolutions from both Parts 1 and 2 as a way to discuss the new school year. The two parts fit together. Everything you do as a parent should have an underlying concern for the effect on the child's self-esteem. For example, if you resolve to spend more time with your child (Part 1, Parent Resolution 7), resolve also to spend that time in a way that interests your child (Part 2, Parent Resolution 9). School success, character growth, and discipline are all related to a positive self-esteem.

Don't try to change your lives completely in order to put all of these resolutions into action. Children can be overwhelmed by too many issues and too many corrections at one time. Besides, families today are busy and there is only enough time for the most important issues. You will need to set priorities and choose a few specific resolutions that are compatible with your own family situation. Work on several items each month. Post the resolutions where you can all see them easily and often. Once a month get together to see how you are doing. Discuss what needs to be added or changed. Make your household into a caring, listening, responsible, co-operative home.

Resolve to have a good year!

The Thinking Parent

Do you feel that your child is out to get you? Never fear! You aren't alone! That's why people like me can write books on the subject. To make you feel better about your parenting efforts and to end this book on a reassuring note, here is a simple acrostic taken from the theme of the book.

Think first. Think about what you have learned from this book. Think about how your child feels, how other family members feel, and how you feel. Think about the response you really want to give and whether it will have positive or negative results.

Hope in heaven's name that you're on the right track! "This isn't really me! That sob sounds like the strange sounds Mom used to make when she accidentally locked herself in the basement when I was a kid!"

Imagine yourself somewhere else—anywhere else! Then go there! Take care of yourself! Parental sanity is important!

Now or never! You've got to get this child into shape and you'll never do it by putting off your action plan. But how can you imagine and go somewhere else if you have to act now? Well, the problem is that the word "think" isn't spelled t-h-n-i-k. Just misspell it in your heads. Then use the guidelines in that order.

Kids! There are 27 million elementary kids in the United States. Many of them survive their parents (and their parents survive *them*). They are kooky, love kruddy slime, kan't sit still, kan't talk without being sassy, and are basically kontrary. But we kan't imagine life without them. Kids will build our history. Kids are our future.

Now, don't you feel better?

Of Related Interest...

SEE HOW THEY GROW
The Early Childhood Years
Dorothy Dixon

Sound, intelligent advice for helping children ages 3-6 make good decisions, as well as understand basic concepts of morals and values.
ISBN: 0-89622-567-4, 96 pp, $7.95

TEACHING YOUNG CHILDREN TO CARE
37 Activities for Developing Self-Esteem
Dorothy Dixon

Helps children consider the question: Who am I? with activities that explore awareness of feelings, wonder at self and nature and a sense of accomplishment.
ISBN: 0-89622-436-8, 88pp, $9.95

TEACHING YOUNG CHILDREN TO CARE
37 Activities for Developing Concern for Others
Dorothy Dixon

Helps children understand the question: Who are you? with topics and role-playing designed to develop a sense of other people's feelings and concerns.
ISBN: 0-89622-437-6, 88 pp, $9.95

VISION 23
A Division of Twenty-Third Publications
P.O. Box 180 • Mystic, CT 06355
1-800-321-0411